THE ENNEAGRAM AND NLP

A Journey of Evolution

Anné Linden
Murray Spalding

Metamorphous Press
Portland, OR

Published by

Metamorphous Press
P.O. Box 10616
Portland, OR 97296-0616

Copyright © 1994 by Anné Linden and Murray Spalding
Editorial and Art Direction by Lori Stephens
Printed in the United States
ISBN 1-55552-042-1

Linden, Anné, 1934-
    The enneagram and NLP : a journey of evolution / Anné Linden, Murray Spalding.
        p.   cm.
    Includes bibliographical references.
    ISBN 1-55552-042-1 : $15.95
    1. Enneagram. 2. Neurolinguistic programming. 3. Typology (Psychology) 4. Psychotherapy. I. Spalding, Murray, 1944-
    II. Title.
    BF698.35.E54L56   1994
    155.2 ' 6--cd20   94-18786

DEDICATION

We dedicate this book to all our clients and students
who have enlightened and nurtured us.

ACKNOWLEDGMENTS

We gratefully acknowledge all those students, clients, colleagues, teachers and friends who supported and encouraged us with challenges and ideas.

Special thanks and appreciation go to Kathleen Riordan-Speeth and Helen Palmer whose work and writings have formed the foundation of our knowledge of the Enneagram.

We also want to thank Susan James, who contributed several case histories; Wyatt Woodsmall, Greig O'Dea, and Jean Moshofsky for sharing their knowledge; and Ellen Cohen and Jim Bleakley, whose comments helped to clarify many points.

And a special acknowledgment and appreciation to Peter Skinner who edited this manuscript with diligence and expertise.

AUTHORS' NOTES

As a teacher and therapist, I spend most of my time working with people, guiding them toward enhanced autonomy, empowerment, choice, and personal and professional success. When one's work involves large numbers of people, one inevitably thinks in terms of commonalities and patterns. The typologies that I had previously learned were unsatisfactory because they were either too rigid or too vague in the way that they categorized people to be useful.

In 1987, I heard someone speak briefly about the Enneagram. I was intrigued! Since then, I have studied the Enneagram and used it in my therapeutic work, and in 1990, I began to teach it as a part of a Self-Esteem Training I have designed. More recently, because of the extraordinary interest it has aroused, I am teaching a synthesis of the Enneagram and NLP as a separate workshop.

For years I had been searching for a cosmology that would describe NLP in relationship to our mental, emotional and spiritual development. The Enneagram seems to be that cosmology—the answer to my search. I have found the Enneagram to be particularly effective and satisfying when used as an overall organizing principle in my therapeutic work. In addition to maintaining my own private practice, I am responsible for the supervision of six to eight therapists at my clinic that uses NLP as a short-term solution- and process-oriented therapy. I introduced these therapists to the Enneagram in 1989, and since that time we have incorporated it as our general organizing frame while using the NLP approach for the specifics in our practice of therapy. All of us have found that this marriage has profoundly enriched, deepened, and enhanced our therapeutic work.

With the Enneagram we can better understand where people are in their journey of evolution and recognize the steps they need to take to continue evolving and growing. It assists us in structuring our therapeutic interventions, creating tasks to shift clients' preoccupations and in general directing their progress, while adding a deeper and broader perspective and understanding to our work.

The Enneagram has opened numerous doors of awareness on a personal level by helping me to identify my weaknesses (challenges) and passions, and transform them into opportunities to learn and evolve. Professionally, I am very excited and enthusiastic about the potential that the Enneagram and NLP offer the therapist and the person interested in pursuing more actively and consciously his/her journey of personal evolution.

I have known Murray for over eight years. Our relationship as fellow professionals began when she studied NLP with me; it continued as we shared observations as therapists, and it eventually became a valued friendship. This book was born over dinner one night as we talked about how the Enneagram was becoming a central focus in our professional and personal lives. It occurred to us that somewhere in our relationship an unwritten book sought tangible form. As the ideas and words flowed between us, it seemed natural and inevitable to put them down on paper. And so . . . this book! May you the reader enjoy and appreciate yourself and your journey a little bit more!

Anné Linden

As co-author of *The Enneagram and NLP*, I found myself on an archeological dig. Time and again while covering old ground, I discovered new intricacies. My past experiences and my present processes of integrating the me of today with the me of yesterday and tomorrow continued with heightened intensity. This book is not a "how to" with easy fix-it answers but rather an exploration of two dynamic systems interwoven to enhance self-awareness and evolution.

For much of my professional life, I have been a dancer, choreographer and director of my own modern dance touring company. During a decade and a half, I created thirty danceworks and toured twenty-six states and Mexico. I still consider myself a dancer, and the creation of dance pieces is one of my passions. As I acquired perspective on the choreography I created, I realized that the intention behind my works was to promote change and awareness. Even after a rigorous performance and sustaining applause, I found myself truly pleased when an audience member came backstage and discussed with me how my choreography affected him/her in a personal way. This one-on-one exchange led me into the field of therapy.

As a therapist, I am constantly confronted with challenges from my clients. Their concerns and desired life changes spark my creativity. I often say to my clients that I am just a fisherman baiting the hook of my comments until the right switch is released and the light bulb of realization is turned on. Indeed, it is a dance—of fearless innovations and interventions.

In my experience, no method or theory has been as successful in affecting breakthroughs and healing as the marriage of the ancient typology system, the Enneagram, and Neuro-Linguistic Programming. Each system is complex; each individually affords greater understanding of human beings and their behaviors. When the two methodologies are combined, understood in depth, and conjointly applied, profound self-realization and evolution is imminent.

I was introduced to the Enneagram in the mid-1970s in Oscar Ichazo's ARICA-Forty Day Program. My more thorough understanding of the system evolved in my discussions with my sister, Greig O'Dea, one of Helen Palmer's first Enneagram teachers and most diligent researchers for Helen's book, *The Enneagram*.

In my process of becoming a therapist, I discovered NLP and its enlightening methods for transformation. After experiencing many inferior teachers of this system, I came upon Anné—a brilliant teacher. Years later, after one of our "Dinner with André" evenings, she asked me to join her in writing this book. Our collaboration has been fun, creative, and an intimately valued dance of the minds.

Murray Spalding

TABLE OF CONTENTS

FOREWORD

Our aim in this book is to bring together the Enneagram (an ancient typology that proposes nine basic personality types), and Neuro-Linguistic Programming (NLP—a psychology of *inter-* and *intrapersonal* intelligence and communication that provides a solution- and process-oriented approach to therapy) in a synthesis that offers a simple way to organize and understand both these disciplines.

For therapists, this combination of therapeutic disciplines will expand their understanding of their clients and provide a system of interventions for change; for those interested in improving their self-esteem and relationships with others, it offers an invaluable guide for self-awareness and growth. This book demonstrates how these two powerful models can enrich each other. "The whole is greater than the sum of its parts" certainly applies to the focused use of the Enneagram in combination with NLP.

THE ENNEAGRAM AND NLP

xiv

PART I

2   THE ENNEAGRAM AND NLP

Chapter 1

Integrating the Enneagram and NLP

The Enneagram is an ancient typology based upon a nine-pointed star (from the Greek: ennea-gram, meaning nine-pointed) which organizes nine personality types within a circle and main triangle. The Enneagram is a powerful guide to self-awareness and evolution, providing it is not used as an instrument of judgment and self-righteousness. Combining it with NLP empowers both models, especially in terms of the models assisting in personal evolution. In summary, knowledge of NLP, when enhanced through awareness of the Enneagram styles of personality, offers the psychotherapist and interested layperson a powerful, fully integrated method for gaining self-awareness and awareness of others.

In brief, NLP is the study of how each individual represents and experiences his/her world uniquely through different patterns and sensory filters. One person may have a finely attuned auditory system, and when viewing a film may be highly attentive to the sounds and music and to what is being said. Another person may experience the film through the kinesthetic system and might report primarily on feelings about the characters or the story. A third person who is visually oriented may comment on the beauty of the scenery or the detail of the sets where the film takes place. Each person's view is different and represents a process by which he/she creates a personal reality.

The Enneagram system reveals even more about how we are each unique. This system asserts that there are nine styles of personality. Each individual's orientation to feeling, thinking and doing varies according to that individual's personality style. For example, a Two Enneagram Style, "The Pleaser-Caretaker," is a feeling type, filtering events and interactions through emotions. Twos utilize the kinesthetic system and use predicates such as *to feel out,* to *get a hold of,* to *touch on,* to *come to grips with.*

This book identifies for each Enneagram style the specific NLP patterns characteristic of it. Through this combination, each system adds to the other by providing a fuller spectrum of understanding about the individual's process and subjective reality. In learning that each of us views and experiences life differently with varying beliefs and criteria, we open doors to fewer judgments and greater forgiveness toward ourselves and others. These personality styles, beliefs, criteria and patterning are developed early in childhood. They serve as a method to protect the self or ego-personality. Each style, often called a fixation, is a strategy for survival. Individuals usually meet attempts at change with resistance because these changes in patterns and beliefs threaten this ego-personality survival strategy. Breaking through the limitations of a fixation allows the self to forge the path of evolution. The use of the Enneagram combined with NLP can increase our capacities for intimacy, creativity, spirituality and empathy—the goal of evolution being paramount for humankind.

We are all trapped inside our own models of the world. The Enneagram provides a key to increased awareness of self. It illuminates and challenges our presuppositions of ourselves and uncovers the games we play. We become aware of our preoccupations and this in turn enlightens our choices. The Enneagram enables us to understand the steps we need to take, the shifts in attention we need to make to continue and inform our personal evolution.

While NLP gives us the specific tools to help achieve these steps and make the shifts, more important, it provides a non-judgmental attitude that enriches the Enneagram and its value to humanity. NLP teaches us how to do non-polar thinking; thinking that is not based on the poles of right/wrong, good/bad, but on observations and options. Our preoccupations and passions are not good or bad. The crucial question is whether we are moving toward balance, which is fluid. As soon as balance is achieved, it changes.

The Sufis, who are thought to have originated the Enneagram system, believed that a person's gifts were the most dangerous of pitfalls because we tend to identify too much with what we consider our strengths, what we do well, and never look at the other side of these gifts, or consider the imbalance inherent within them. For example, in the Enneagram system, Eights are considered to be strong personalities; indeed, Eights pride themselves on their strength. But this very gift of strength can prevent them from acknowledging their vulnerability and weaknesses and, as a result, they limit their true evolution.

Identifying our core type opens a door onto the landscape of our preoccupations and obsessions, our tendencies, desires and fears, and our beliefs. This identification is a guide to our basic and potential personalities. Everyone of us is on a journey of evolution. The Enneagram is the road map that greatly informs and helps us to manage this journey. NLP allows us to use this information to evolve ourselves more profoundly with greater focus, precision, and elegance.

Knowledge and informed and non-judgmental utilization of the Enneagram also help us to truly understand others; providing the vehicle to put aside our ego and step into another's shoes and to become that other, without losing our independence. This expands our compassion and extends our understanding beyond identification.

The key to using the Enneagram is acceptance without judgment—you *are* evolving and there is no limit to the possibilities of your potential. Sometimes, when people first identify which type they are, they say, "Perhaps I can evolve to another type." This indicates that they are judging one type to be better than another. Not so! Within each type there are levels of evolution: less evolved, evolved, more highly evolved—and our level of evolution can vary in different contexts.

Our type is the theme that remains constant throughout our life while the possibilities for physical, mental, emotional and spiritual evolution are limitless. With NLP skills and technology we can use the information gained from knowledge of our type to develop those patterns that do not come naturally and direct our attention to choices other than the ones we seem habitually to prefer.

Since our conscious attention is consistently limited to between five and nine pieces of information at any moment (7 plus or minus 2; George Miller, 1950s), shifting our attention from habitual modes can have the same effect as shifting the direction of a flashlight in a darkened room—illuminating dark corners, increasing our input of information about this room, our understanding of the nature of its space and our choices of what can be done in it and how to use it.

Developing choices in our major perceptual filters, our cognitive filters, cognitive processes, cognitive qualifiers, frames of reference, and chunking enhance our ability to evolve and grow. (For definitions of these NLP terms, see Appendix 1: Glossary.)

Depending upon the Enneagram personality type, a relatively simple shift from matching to mismatching, from attention to the kinesthetic system to attention to the visual, or changing the way one chunks can profoundly affect and significantly advance personal evolution. NLP provides the specific "how to's" for changing these patterns, and for making evolution more concrete, achievable and responsive to personal awareness and responsibility. Personal evolution then becomes more of a choice within one's control, rather than some mysterious and seemingly accidental, incidental process of osmosis.

The ability to identify one's own and others' Enneagram types, even though difficult, can be learned by attending to certain patterns and issues, and the way a person handles them. For example, take issues such as control, commitment, authority, success, anger, fear. Each type responds to these issues in very different ways. Consider control: Ones control through self-righteousness; Twos control through love—loving someone so well that you become indispensable; Threes control by constantly doing—always keeping busy and achieving; Fours control through emotional drama; Fives control by withdrawal, or non-reaction; Sixes control through paranoia; Sevens control through jumping from one option to another; Eights control by confrontation and fighting; Nines control by slowing down.

To provide a comprehensive account of integrating the Enneagram and NLP, this book includes a brief history and summary of both the Enneagram and NLP; a description of each of the Enneagram's Nine Personality Types with vignettes and case histories; and a series of Appendixes that include an Enneagram Quiz; the Identifying Interview; a Glossary of NLP Terms; a collection of NLP Therapeutic Processes and Interventions; and a list of recommended books on NLP and on the Enneagram.

Chapters 3 through 11 present a summary of each of the Nine Personality Types. We have organized these descriptions around specific topics: Aspects of Personality, Childhood Theme, Typical Beliefs, Typical Compelling Questions, Boundary Issues, Shifts of Attention Toward Personal Evolution, Vignettes, Case Histories, Therapeutic Approach, NLP Patterns, and NLP Therapeutic Interventions.

When reading these descriptions, please keep in mind that within each type there are the three possible levels of development: less evolved, evolved and highly evolved, and that these can change from one context to another, and from the past, present and future. As you read these descriptions you may recognize aspects of yourself that were true in the past, are true now or may be true in the future. This is simply an indication of your evolution and represents the growth you have already achieved and the challenge and opportunity for future personal development.

In combining the Enneagram and NLP, this book creates a model for psychotherapy that can be used as a guide by therapists or by interested individuals as an approach to personal evolution. We hope that it will serve you well.

Chapter 2

A Brief History and Summary

The origins of the Enneagram are shrouded in speculation and mystery, due to the oral tradition which passed the concept and its formulation from teacher to student verbally and to the secrecy that surrounded these teachings. There was concern that this information would be ill-used and could be damaging in the wrong hands. For several hundred years, knowledge of the Enneagram was preserved and taught as a spiritual practice; in fact, it was not until the 1980s that books on the Enneagram began to be published. Now this system is being widely written about and taught.

Although some historians speculate that the Enneagram may have originated up to 5,000 years ago in Babylon, most people accept that the Enneagram had its beginning in medieval mathematical discoveries. It appeared in the Middle East during the fifteenth century when Islamic mathematicians discovered the power and the meaning of the number zero and developed the decimal system which is used throughout the world today. The Sufis, who were Islamic mystics, then combined these mathematical figures with their knowledge of the dynamics of the human spirit to create the present day symbol of the Enneagram. They called it the "Face of God." Whatever the Enneagram's specific origins were, George Ivanovitch Gurdjieff, the famed 20th century spiritual teacher, is responsible for bringing knowledge of this system to the West. It was passed on through small study groups, and some mention of the Enneagram appears in the writing of P. D. Ouspenski, a student of Gurdjieff's.

The Franciscans and Jesuits seem to have been influenced by the Enneagram as early as the 17th century and certainly in the later half of the 20th century. The Jesuits have taught and utilized it widely.

Oscar Ichazo, founder of Arica Institute, further expanded and developed the system and began to teach it in Chile during the 1960s. He continued his teachings in the United States after he moved to New York in 1971. Among his American students were John Lilly, M.D., Kathleen Riordan-Speeth, and the psychiatrist Claudio Naranjo. Until the early 1970s, all teaching was done orally; then there began to appear written informal notes that were passed around at various seminars given by Kathleen Riordan-Speeth. In the 1980s, formal studies began to be published. (Appendix 6 includes a partial listing of books on the Enneagram.)

Since the Enneagram is a typology of human personality, it is relevant to briefly mention four other analogous typologies: first, astrology, which has a structure based upon the zodiac— the twelve sun signs and the location and movement of the sun, moon, and planets at the time of birth; second, Jungian typology, which has three pairs of functions—introversion/extroversion, perception/intuition, thinking/feeling; third, the Myers-Briggs system which includes the three types of Jungian functions and adds a fourth: judging/perceiving—it combines these eight into sixteen possible types; and fourth, Karen Horney postulated a typology based upon three different ways people try to overcome their fear of life: submission (turning to others), hostility (aggression against others), and withdrawal (isolation from others); and four ways through which people attempt to protect themselves from fundamental anxiety: love, submissiveness, power, and withdrawal.

The symbols of the triangle and circle, the star and the number 3, which are basic to the depiction of the Enneagram, have been used in many religions and schools of philosophy. Among the related figures are the Star of David, the Tree of Life of the Cabala, the Major Arcana of the Tarot and the Jungian Archetypal Figures.

As a typology of human personality, the Enneagram presents a structure for a profound and evolutionary understanding of ourselves and others. In the animal kingdom, each species exhibits certain similarities that serve to define that particular species, but each species also has numerous differences. Similarly, each of the Enneagram's nine personality types exhibit consistent commonalities, but also have room for unique individual traits.

This typology is a map of human differences and similarities, postulating nine distinct personality types. Each core personality type is influenced by its wing points that lie to either side of the core type (see diagram, p. 13) and moves to aspects of another personality type in stress, and to yet another in security. Stress must not invariably be thought of as negative, nor security as positive. Stress can be positive and security can be negative, depending upon the context and the individual. That is, a person can move to these aspects as needed and use them as resources or pitfalls. When moving to these points the individual can draw upon either the evolved or less evolved aspects of the type. This movement becomes habitual and creates a multidimensional picture of each individual. For example, each Two is unique. A Two who is an executive may often move to Eight in order to draw upon the leadership aspects of an Eight to facilitate projects. This is not in reaction to stress as a negative state.

As the diagram indicates, wings are the points that lie to either side of the core type, variations of the personality influencing and flavoring each type. The wing that influences each core personality type and the extent of this influence are extremely idiosyncratic. For example, an Eight can be influenced by aspects of the Nine or the Seven, or be more purely Eight with little influence from either wing. Another way to think about this concept is to imagine that the circle is made up of a series of dots and that each person falls upon one of these dots. The point at which he/she falls may be half way between two types or closer to a particular type. Where one falls determines the extent of the influence of an individual's wing. As each type moves to aspects of another at different periods in life and in different contexts, these flow patterns become familiar over time. Unlike other typologies, this movement goes beyond rigidity or generalized vagueness to achieve a more dynamic balance. Thus each person retains individual uniqueness within the frame of one of the nine personality types.

In addition to the wings and points of stress and security, Enneagram scholars subtype each personality type as **sexual** (oriented toward one-on-one); **social** (oriented toward groups); or **self-preservation** (oriented toward self). For example, at a party a Two who is a sexual sub-type is more seductive and comfortable connecting to one other person. A Two who is a social subtype is concerned with everyone getting along. A Two who is a self-preservation subtype enters the party and heads for the food and drink.

We have chosen not to elaborate on this dimension of the Enneagram because it would complicate an already complex and subtle system and obscure the connections between the Enneagram and NLP.

Within the Enneagram's nine personality types, there are three triads that share certain similarities. For people in the Two, Three and Four triad the central issue is **identity** (who am I?); their center of intelligence is the **heart** and their basic defense is **toward**. They don't know **who** they are; they think through their emotions, and defend themselves by moving toward acceptance and approval. Their relationship to the issue of safety/security being tied up with identity often results in their having no boundaries. (See Appendix 1, Glossary of NLP Terms.) For those in the Five, Six and Seven triad the central issue is **fear**; their center of intelligence is the **head** and their basic defense is **away from**. They respond out of fear; they filter experience through mental activities and defend selves by going away from personal involvement and intimacy. Their relationship to the issue of safety/security being tied up with fear often results in their having walls. For those in the Eight, Nine and One triad the central issue is **anger**; their center of intelligence is the **gut** and their basic defense is **against**. They respond to the world from anger, either overtly or covertly; they think through their instincts, and defend themselves by fighting against control and vulnerability. Their relationship to the issue of safety/security being tied up with anger often results in their bouncing back and forth between having no boundaries or having walls.

Usually by the time a person is three years of age, his/her core type can be identified; in fact, the type is often evident at

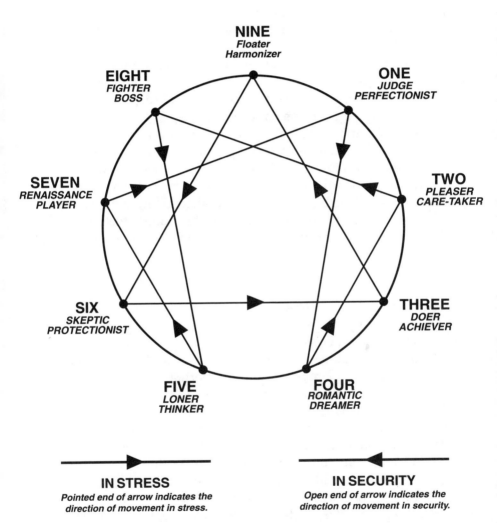

IN STRESS
*Pointed end of arrow indicates the
direction of movement in stress.*

IN SECURITY
*Open end of arrow indicates the
direction of movement in security.*

NOTE: The way that each individual defines and gives meaning
to the words Stress and Security is idiosyncratic. Stress
is not necessarily experienced as negative and security is
not necessarily experienced as positive.

birth or soon after. Although an individual remains his/her type throughout life, the potential for evolution is limited only by time, awareness, and desire. The more highly evolved the person becomes, the more access he/she has to the useful aspects of all the other types—while remaining in essence true to the core type.

The purists feel that the soul is a clean slate, coming into life without an ego personality type. Through interaction with parents, early life at home, and accumulating experience, the personality type is set by seven years of age.

The more metaphysical opinion contends that the soul consciously chooses his/her ego type for its ultimate evolution in the present lifetime and is a specific personality at birth. Depending upon the environment and upon parents and society, innate strengths can be enhanced or weakened and weaknesses magnified or diminished. The patterns of thinking, feeling and doing of each type are lessons unique to each soul's experience.

* * * * *

In direct contrast to the Enneagram, Neuro-Linguistic Programming (NLP) is a strictly contemporary psychotherapeutic tool and discipline.

NLP was developed by Richard Bandler and John Grinder in the mid-1970s. Combining their expertise in mathematics, computer science and linguistics they created a model of human behavior. This was done by modeling the ancestors of NLP: Milton H. Erickson, M.D., Gregory Bateson, Virginia Satir and Fritz Perls. Modeling is a process of observing and eliciting **how** someone does something—the specific behavioral steps and their sequence. Erickson, Satir and Perls were master communicators, and Bandler and Grinder discovered how they achieved the results they did. These discoveries, plus some of the basic concepts underlying Erickson's and Bateson's work form the foundation of NLP.

NLP encompasses the three most influential components involved in producing human experience: neurology, language, and programming. The neurological system regulates how our bodies function, and language determines the kinds of models of the world we create. NLP describes the fundamental dynamics between mind (neuro) and language (linguistic), and how their interaction affects our body, emotions and behavior (programming).

NLP is a psychology of **inter**personal and **intra**personal intelligence and communication that addresses the many levels involved in being human. It is a multi-dimensional epistemology that includes the specific delineation and examination of the perceptual and cognitive processes that produce behavior, thinking and emotion. At another level, NLP is about self-discovery, identity and one's personal mission in life. It provides a framework for understanding and relating to the spiritual part of human experience that reaches beyond us as individuals to our family, community and global systems.

These foundations of NLP are best summed up in the **Presuppositions of NLP:**

• **The meaning of your communication is the response you get, independent of your intention.** This does not mean intentions are unimportant; they are crucial to the true establishment of respect and rapport. However, when interacting with another human being it is essential that you take responsibility for **your** communication by determining its effectiveness based upon the response of the other, rather than on what you intended. This allows for the creation of a cybernetic loop which generates a more dynamic type of communication; rather than the linear, more static ping-pong effect.

• **There is a positive intention or purpose behind all behavior.** This positive intention occurs at the **intra**personal, rather than the **inter**personal level. Any behavior—external, or internal, such as talking to oneself or making images—is trying to take care of the person (as determined by that person's unconscious) in some way.

• **People have sufficient resources to accomplish whatever they want** (providing accomplishment is possible in this world). People have the inner resources to develop other resources, abilities, attitudes, skills, knowledge and to utilize available external resources.

• **The map is not the territory.** Our perception of reality is not reality—only our individual representation of it. Just as a map is but a representation of an actual geographic area, our map of the world is our unique representation of the world.

• **Failure is not failure, it's feedback.** Failure and mistakes are labels we give to circumstances where we do not get the results we want. When we utilize failure as an opportunity to learn, to get more or different information, we increase our chances of success the next time or the time after that.

• **People make the best choices available to them at the time.** For something to be a choice it must be doable, immediately available and effective. Given our perceptions of our experiences we do the best we can, under the circumstances.

• **Choices are desirable and there are many.** There are as many choices as points of view. One option is no choice, two is a dilemma, and three is choice.

• **Empowerment is the ability to produce intended results.** To know what you want, what that will look like, sound like and feel like; to develop the skills and strategies to accomplish it, and to move in the direction of your personal and professional goals is being truly powerful.

Because of the scientific fact that our conscious mind can only pay attention to between five and nine pieces of information at a time, the NLP concept of **Representational Systems** and how they effect our behavior and emotions becomes even more significant. These systems are the building blocks of experience and relate to our five sensory systems: **visual, auditory, kinesthetic** (primary/sensation and emotions), **olfactory** and **gustatory**. Given that we cannot pay conscious attention to even a fraction of the stimuli available in any experience, we filter all perceptual and sensory information, deleting a tremendous amount in order not to become overwhelmed. The sensory system we pay most conscious attention to is formed because of exposure to and stimulation of that particular system. We delete sensory systems because of associations to painful experiences or lack of stimulation. After we've been exposed to an experience, we represent (remember/think about) that experience via a specific Representational System: the sensory system we use to represent a specific thought, desire, memory.

Examining the sensory system that dominates our thinking in specific situations and the qualities of that system we favor allows us to understand and shift our thinking, memories, planning and goal-setting in ways that are beneficial and give us more control—choice, that is in the use of our minds.

The emphasis in NLP is on the process of experience—the **how**, rather than the **why**, and this has led to discoveries of the finer distinctions in internal and external behavior that make seemingly inexplicable behavior or emotions logical and understandable. This increased awareness takes the mystery out of change and makes it more easily attainable.

Whether we want to solve a problem, learn how someone does something well, or achieve a goal, we ask the question, "How is it possible that (I, he/she can/cannot . . .)?"

NLP therapy and communication concentrates on **process** rather than **content**, on **how** rather than **why**, and focuses on the **outcomes** rather than **problems**. Through conscious design, NLP provides a structure to examine both our **intra**personal experience and our **inter**personal experience in order to discover the specific step by step process that is occurring, thereby giving us the tools to adjust or change either our inner world or the way we interact with another.

NLP emphasizes non-polar thinking (polar: good/bad, right/wrong); the ability to observe, gather and analyze information, and interact with another **without** judgment. Using certain NLP patterns and skills, non-polar thinking becomes more doable and a conscious choice. Combining non-polar thinking with curiosity, directing conscious attention toward the external world (which then bypasses the ego), and having compassion for another human being create the position of Fair Witness. This position is non-judgmental but **not** detached or aloof. It is involved but not directed toward helping the other—only being there with energy and compassion/empathy toward the ultimate humanness of another—not whether he/she achieves the goal or solves the problem. Fair Witness is the most ecological position to assume when studying and using the Enneagram. (See Appendix 4, p. 167, for more detailed information regarding the Fair Witness Position.)

In summary, NLP has been developed on the premise that there is a certain knowable logic and sequence that underlie the mental activity that regulates and produces all emotions and behaviors. While this sequence is different for every individual, it is nonetheless knowable by every individual. This knowledge increases choices and increases the possibility of humans achieving their positive potential. As Milton Erickson always emphasized, the therapist should create the intervention to fit the client, rather than trying to make the client fit the intervention. Using the cosmology of the Enneagram and the concepts and tools of NLP, the therapist can transform this knowledge into experience.

In the Enneagram, the criterion of survival formulates the personality type; in NLP the most highly valued criterion is survival of self and loved ones. This shared belief system creates a natural marriage between the Enneagram and NLP psychotherapy.

ONE: THE JUDGE-PERFECTIONIST

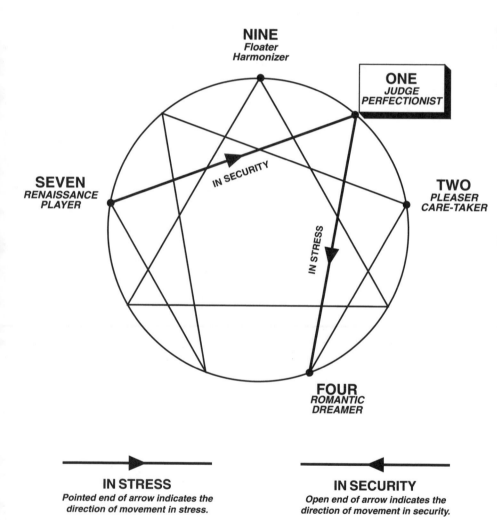

IN STRESS
*Pointed end of arrow indicates the
direction of movement in stress.*

IN SECURITY
*Open end of arrow indicates the
direction of movement in security.*

NOTE: The way that each individual defines and gives meaning
to the words Stress and Security is idiosyncratic. Stress
is not necessarily experienced as negative and security is
not necessarily experienced as positive.

Chapter 3

ONE: THE JUDGE-PERFECTIONIST

Ones are the Judge-Perfectionists of the Enneagram System. Their wing is either the Floater-Harmonizer (Nine) or the Pleaser-Caretaker (Two). When in stress they move to the Romantic-Dreamer (Four) and when in security they move to the Renaissance-Player (Seven). They are chiefly concerned with perfection and avoidance of anger—a sort of angry virtue or rigid self-righteousness. Their primary defense is anger turned inward. Anger and the expression of it is their basic issue. **Ones** will censor their anger and express it indirectly through criticism and dissatisfaction toward self and others. Their center of intelligence is the gut—being fundamentally instinctual thinkers. Their most comfortable style of being is thinking.

Main Filter or Focus of Attention: What's right or wrong in any situation.

Childhood Theme/Concern: Be good in order to stay out of trouble. They experienced being criticized or punished a lot, had premature adult responsibility, and were rarely rewarded.

Personality Traits: Ones have high standards and principles, are idealistic, and are moral heroes/heroines. They have personal and moral integrity, are ambitious, reliable, respectable, loyal and hard workers. There is one correct way for them and they are more comfortable thinking rather than feeling. They take care of and are compassionate toward those less fortunate than themselves. They repress feelings of their own wants, and need to be in control of their environment, often with obsessive compulsive needs of orderliness or excessive cleanliness. They have a tendency toward dichotomous, polar thinking—either/ or, black or white, no grays—this creates rigidity and a lack of flexibility. They have a strong internal critical voice with lots of "shoulds" and "musts"—critical of self and others. The superego dominates so that they always think they know how it should be and how it should be done. Constantly moving toward perfection, they are often not in touch with feelings, including anger which is then expressed as irritation, resentment, indignation and guilt. There is a sense of two selves: the controlled self that cannot let go and the secret self wanting or doing what they most condemn in others. **Ones** are seldom satisfied with themselves and experience few options or lighthearted fun. They often procrastinate for fear of making a mistake; taking a chance is difficult because of their need to be perfect, to avoid imperfection at all costs.

Typical Beliefs: I'm/things are never good enough. Nothing is ever good enough. I don't deserve. Pleasure and happiness must be earned and deserved. You have to suffer. If things are easy, they're not worthwhile.

Typical Compelling Question: "Am I good enough?" "What's wrong with this?" "What should be done?" "Am I in control?" "Have I done enough?"

Boundary Issues: Walls rather than permeable boundaries between mind, body and feeling. Loss of self-other boundaries in intimate relationships.

Attention Shifts for Personal Evolution: Ones' evolution is enhanced by the development of boundaries (permeable separation) and flexibility, shifting modal operators of necessity (shoulds) to possibility (wants), strengthening appreciation of self and others, and increasing the balance between thinking and feeling. You can humanize and expand your high standards for self and others and develop the belief, "I'm perfectly human, and that is good enough." Make real the presupposition that "There is no such thing as failure, only feedback," by incorporating it into your behavior and belief systems.

Specifics: Develop the choice to do non-polar/optional thinking rather than polar thinking. Match self—what you do and have. Change "shoulds" to "wants." Sort more by people. Become more proactive, especially regarding self and own wants. Cultivate positive and acceptable counter-examples to standard of perfection. Create boundaries between thinking (head) and emotions (heart). Recognize and direct appropriate expression of anger. Appreciate others' values that are different from yours. Witness, adjust, and develop more choices with internal critical voices. Cultivate the value of patience and a sense of humor about yourself and the world.

VIGNETTES

Jane I. is a successful professional in her mid-thirties. When she first came into therapy, she had been fasting—drinking only bouillon and juices for over a year—in order to have a perfect body. Eating meant a loss of control to Jane. After therapy work on her belief, "Feeling and expressing my emotions will make me lose control and if I lose control I'll go crazy," she became willing to relate to food again. Initially she gained weight, but as she was able to recognize and express her emotions, she began to eat in a healthy way and her weight stabilized.

* * * * *

Bettina R., an intelligent successful business woman in her late twenties, was aware and evolving and had done a lot of self improvement trainings and workshops. However, she constantly came down on herself for not improving fast enough and well enough. When her standard of perfection was challenged, she objected strenuously, "I want to be perfect; I will NOT give up perfection." At that moment someone said to her, "Remember you're perfectly human!" This remark caught her attention and put her in a paradoxical bind between her standard of perfection and the fact of being human. This double bind began to shake her loose from her absolute, polar position regarding perfection and she began to accept the possibilities of options—even in relationship to her cherished perfection.

* * * * *

Leon V., a psychoanalyst in his fifties with a well-known reputation, was a member of a professional organization. He perceived himself as the ultimate authority on what psychoanalysis was and who was really practicing "correctly." He accused anyone who presented an "interesting" idea of which he had not thought of not doing psychoanalysis. Because of Leon V.'s reputation, he initially intimidated people and his censure was not questioned. Gradually, as he continued to find fault with others and condemn any new and different idea or style as not being real psychoanalysis, his influence began to wane. He believed there was a right way to do psychoanalysis and it was his responsibility to keep it true and pure! This psychoanalyst is an example of self-righteous rigidity and an unevolved **One**.

CASE HISTORIES

Rita S. is a thinking type whose daily decisions are determined by "right or wrong," "good or bad," "fair or not fair." Rita is an older lady, mother and housewife. Her process of thinking is very polar. She gave her children and her home her strict supervision and meticulous attention and time.

Her home is *House and Garden* perfect. She chose each antique with care and coordinated the colors with a decorator's flair. She speaks of her children as if they were objects. Rita once commented on her eldest child, saying that he had been very "satisfactory" from the moment of birth. This is a client who is tremendously critical of others as well as herself. She holds an ideal of what is correct and finds it difficult to understand why others do not think precisely the way she does. After all, they "should" since she is correct. In one session, Rita S. commented, "I felt so good when I was arguing with my daughter-in-law, because I knew I was right." It never occurred to her to consider her daughter-in-law's feelings.

Rita S. also has difficulty recognizing the impact of her anger on others. She releases anger by lashing out at unsuspecting persons such as the taxi driver, the waitress, or the telephone solicitor. The true well of anger is inappropriately directed and the critical self has a difficult time forgiving.

Rita S. is oriented to small details and information. She is a master at mismatching; she will willingly comment on a picture hanging askew in the office or on the absence of a pillow from the office couch.

Rita S.'s tendency towards perfection allows her little fun. Her belief system always implicitly asks more and more of herself and others. Nothing is quite enough. As one of her children commented when in a joint session, "I can't do enough—when visiting, it is never long enough, or when helping to clean up, she follows behind doing it better."

The therapy work with Rita S. has centered on awareness of her own behavior and how it affects others. She is slowly getting in touch with her own deeper feelings and recognizing the power of her words and the anger behind them. Teaching Rita S. the **Perceptual Positions Process** has given her more choice in how to deal with her anger. She is becoming aware of the powerful impact of her tone of voice and is more sensitive to others. Being right and being the perfect mother-in-law has become less important than the feelings of others.

* * * * *

Diane L. is a 63-year-old woman who entered therapy initially complaining of depression. Discussion quickly revealed an extremely rigid, angry, authoritarian stance vis-a-vis her co-workers which did little to earn their liking or respect. Her depression, however, was the result of her self-righteousness and her determination to maintain it even at the risk of total isolation and alienation. This depression stemmed from chronic rage and helplessness about her inability to convince others of the error of their ways, and she came to therapy wanting help. She believed that it was only to be expected that others would view her as a self-righteous, hostile, critical stick-in-the-mud because they were too blind to see that she was doing the right things. Earlier in life, she had been employed in positions of considerable influence and authority, but for various reasons now held a job that was much lower in status and power, and she had never really reconciled herself to this new position. In her current job she became preoccupied with having a tidy desk, paperclips in the right place, etc.

She was in conflict with herself because the "right" way to be did not include being angry, impatient, critical and judgmental. She could only be perfect, yet she wasn't, and so her anger and criticism was as much at herself as anyone else.

The first and most difficult task in therapy was to persuade her to change her outcome for therapy, i.e., to have her consider the possibility that her own attitudes, beliefs and values were contributing to her misery. This task was much easier said than done because from her point of view, she didn't have attitudes, beliefs, values or a point-of-view. Instead she had the absolute truth, for herself and everyone. She had much difficulty giving up the authority and control implicit in having the right and only truth.

She responded well to working with her critical internal voice, and this awareness gave her more of a sense of control and she began to build a more positive inner structure. This change in turn gave her more choice in her interactions with others. She made changes in her inner dialogue that allowed her more flexibility in difficult work situations.

As a result of several **Reframes, Change Histories** and **Reimprinting Processes,** Diane L. gradually began to ease up on herself, develop more flexibility with her standard of perfection, and to make friends with herself. Her family and coworkers responded more positively to her, and she began to enjoy her life more.

THERAPEUTIC APPROACH FOR ONES

Ones' fundamental strategy to deal with their survival and safety is to be right. "If I'm perfect I'll be safe." This creates rigidity, self-righteousness, and dichotomous polar thinking. Their core issue is anger. **Ones'** basic defensive position is against being wrong, and they come from the gut as their center of intelligence—their judgments are instinctual and are then rationalized cognitively.

According to the traditional psychological diagnosis, **Ones** tend toward compulsive-obsessive behaviors, with the emphasis on compulsive. Translated into NLP terms, this behavior relates to a constant critical internal voice and the need to fulfill this criterion of perfection. This need often results in a passivity that prevents any true appreciation of self. In general, **Ones** need guidance to make more dynamic their rigid standard of perfection, establish a more positive and patient relationship with self, develop permeable boundaries between their mind, body, and emotions, and to create a strategy for non-polar thinking.

NLP PATTERNS
(see Appendix 1 for definitions)

Sort by Information

Small Chunk

Mismatch self and others

Model Operators of Necessity: "shoulds & musts"

Universal Quantifiers

Visual

Internal Critical Auditory

Internal Frame of Reference

Passive

Dissociated: from emotion and body

Compare self to idealized self

Polar/Dichotomous Thinking: either/or

Criterion: Perfection

SPECIFIC NLP THERAPEUTIC INTERVENTIONS

As therapists we have found that the progress and evolution of our clients depends upon three categories of development: **Boundaries, Beliefs** and **Criteria**, and **Internal/External Worlds**. Since the Enneagram system is a dynamic one, the limitations and challenges of each personality type fall into issues relating to boundaries; to negative beliefs and conflicting and/or rigid criteria; and to a preoccupation with either the inner or the outer world which results in an imbalance and/or impaired relationship between the two. Therefore we have organized our interventions within these categories.

BOUNDARIES
• Use **Perceptual Positions Process** to give **Ones** more awareness and choice of when, where, and how to deal with their issues and emotions of anger and self-righteousness in their interactions with others.
• Utilize **Change History Process** regarding their experience of being criticized.
• Use the **Boundaries Model** and **Process** regarding their relationship with Self (self-esteem) and significant others.

BELIEFS & CRITERIA
• Challenge **Ones'** definition or complex equivalent for perfection. Use NLP **Criteria Ladder, Counter-Example Utilizations, Re-Prioritization of Criteria**, and the **Spin**.
• Identify **Ones'** beliefs surrounding the issues of "being right, being perfect, being good," "working hard," "controlling oneself and others." Use **Submodality Belief Change Process, Change History** or the **Reimprinting Process** to alter the beliefs that are limiting.
• Use **Fair Witness Process** on the polar thinking. Use **Ones'** Criteria of "being good/better" and "fairness" to realize the limits of polar thinking.

INTERNAL/EXTERNAL WORLDS
• Challenge how **Ones** subordinate fun, pleasure and spontaneity in the present to a future time, which usually means never. Utilize **Timeline** work.
• Utilize the **Spacial Reframe** on Part 1, the strict, moral, controlled self and Part 2, the instinctual, libidinous self. Aim toward balance and communication between the parts. Parts work in general support a more positive self-esteem.
• Challenge **Ones'** use of the modal operator "should" and transform it into "want" and "can." Use the **Self-to-Idealized-Self Process**.
• Encourage physical work to release anger and aggressive feelings.
• Use **Changing Expectations Process** to help them match selves, appreciate what they are doing and what is already there.

• **Reframe (6-Step)** the constant internal auditory voice that criticizes, mismatches self (nothing is good enough) and uses the phrase, "I should . . ."

• Use the concept of **Throughtime** to allow **Ones** to relate to the changes they have made in the past and what is possible in the future. This recognition of change provides the ability to be less rigid and more fluid. Teaching **Ones** to experience themselves more as a process rather than an end product that needs to be perfected may lead to more patience with themselves and to the belief, "The Journey Is All There Is."

TWO: THE PLEASER-CARETAKER

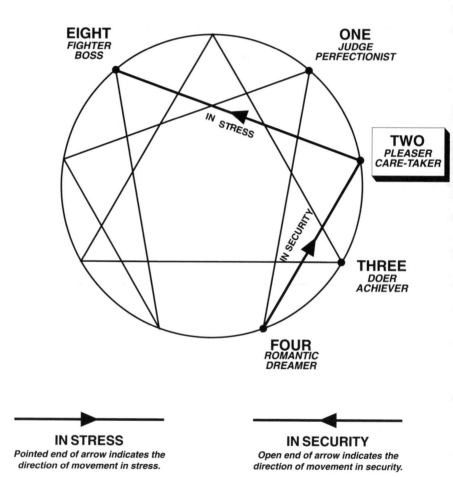

IN STRESS
Pointed end of arrow indicates the direction of movement in stress.

IN SECURITY
Open end of arrow indicates the direction of movement in security.

NOTE: The way that each individual defines and gives meaning to the words Stress and Security is idiosyncratic. Stress is not necessarily experienced as negative and security is not necessarily experienced as positive.

Chapter 4

TWO: THE PLEASER-CARETAKER

Twos are the Pleaser-Caretakers, with a wing either of the Judge-Perfectionist (One) or the Doer-Achiever (Three). They move to the Fighter-Boss (Eight) in stress and to the Romantic-Dreamer (Four) in security. They are chiefly concerned with helping others in order to be loved—a sort of egocentric generosity. **Twos** would rather be seen for what they are, rather than what they do. Like Threes, they tend to repress their own needs, and their chief defense is identification/merging with another and pride in their ability to love and detect what others need. Their basic issue is their identity (Who am I?), and the center of their intelligence is the heart. Their most comfortable style of being is feeling.

Main Filter or Focus of Attention: Approval and acceptance of self from others.

Childhood Theme/Concern: A sense of being loved for pleasing others. **Twos** are considered Mommy or Daddy's good little boy or girl—the "special" child. They sometimes had to take care of parents emotionally; however, there is little cruelty or physical neglect reported. Their sense of self developed from how others reacted to them and a belief that much was expected of them. They experienced getting what they wanted by becoming indispensable.

Personality Traits: People and relationships have high priority with **Twos**. They are gentle, considerate, emotional, productive, dependable, and responsible. Able to bring out the best in others, they are good at flattery and seek flattery themselves. They are attracted to those who are "hard to get" and can be seductive, winsome and vivacious. They become special by pleasing others. It's easier for **Twos** to know what they want when they're alone and independent rather than with others because they habitually sense the wishes and desires of others and yield autonomy, repressing their real wants and needs. Betrayal of their inner self often results in hysteria—outpouring of feelings. **Twos** are prone to somaticize—developing illnesses related to repressed needs and wants. They move toward others' approval, which they seek for their own self-esteem and sense of survival. Attending to others' needs can be a form of manipulation and control in less evolved **Twos**. They can develop a stubborn pride in thinking they know what is best for others. They tend to become the person they think the other wants and will often actually merge with the other without conscious choice. **Twos** trap others and at the same time are trapped. They are good at feeling rather than thinking and have a sense of many selves—sometimes fearing there is no "real self." **Twos** have a dichotomy: merging and freedom. They merge to attain acceptance through love and connection, very often losing their boundaries. They move toward independence to satisfy their need for freedom and boundaries. The dichotomy occurs between the need to merge for acceptance and to be separate for freedom.

Typical Beliefs: Others have to be happy in order for me to be loved. Others' wants/needs are more important than mine. I cannot be separate and be loved.

Typical Compelling Question: "Will I be liked?" "Which one is the real me?" "Do they really love me?"

Boundary Issues: Lack of self/other boundaries—no boundaries between self and important others. They will sometimes polarize to walls in order to protect themselves.

Attention Shifts for Personal Evolution: Twos' evolution revolves around the challenge to develop a stronger internal frame of reference. Accessing and developing your internal visual and auditory systems will contribute to more of a balance between thinking and feeling. You benefit from the choice to recognize your own needs and wants, developing the belief, "I can be separate and connect," "I'm lovable for myself—for who I am." This recognition will support the creation of permeable boundaries between self and others.

Specifics: **Twos** should develop choice to mismatch (emotions and people as well as information), and sort by information! Notice differences between self and others. Develop self-other boundaries. Question desire to please (is it a way to avoid your own wants and needs?) Learn to express anger directly and immediately. Develop choice to say "no" congruently. Strengthen and trust **internal** values.Develop more choices in auditory and visual submodalities. Treat feelings of helplessness as an opportunity to learn and take responsibility for self. Learn to chunk down, appreciating details rather than just large concepts. Challenge own mind reading and develop second position— **Observer Position**.

VIGNETTES

During a supervision session at a therapy clinic, the supervisor was attempting to give feedback to Anne N., one of the therapists. Anne, a **Two,** was resisting the feedback. Finally the supervisor got irritated and commented that Anne seemed unwilling and/or unable to take in her suggestions, "If you disagree with me tell me so directly; otherwise, listen and take it in." Being a **Two,** it was difficult for Anne to take the suggestion, particularly from an authority figure. **Twos** have difficulty with direct confrontation or anger. They can express anger, especially when they go to Eight, but they do not enjoy it like an Eight would. The other issue operating here is that **Twos** truly believe that they know what's best for others (intimate others and those in their care). When Anne's supervisor pointed this out to her, Anne replied with a straight face, "Well, of course I know what's best for my clients!"

* * * * *

I was discussing the Enneagram with some students, and a man who is a **Two** said, "With people who are important to me, I'm very intuitive—I always know what they should do, even when they won't admit it."

* * * * *

A woman in her early fifties who was a student in an NLP training in Paris said when talking about her relationships with men, "I've always had trouble knowing who I am with them— maintaining my independence. I would keep trying to please them—my father, brothers, husband—but somehow I never succeeded." She is a **Two**; people-oriented, nurturing, likes to take care of others and is very kinesthetic/emotional. However, in order to establish boundaries and have some sense of self as a separate being, she decided when very young to become a scientist. This forced her to learn to mismatch, sort by information, and chunk small. These patterns emphasized difference and prevented her from merging with others and losing her boundaries.

CASE HISTORIES

Barbara L. is a dancer who, like many **Twos,** holds the belief that "I am my feelings" and has issues concerning boundaries and need for approval. She is sensitive and dedicated to her dance and to her therapy work. In our first session, Barbara's outcome was to have appropriate boundaries. She was confused about how and when to express her limits with her roommate. She lived in a Soho loft and rented a room from an older man, her landlord and roommate. He left food out on the kitchen counter and dirty dishes in the sink. Almost daily, she found herself cleaning up after him. He never recognized her efforts or gave her any thanks. As she pleaded, "I need courage to speak my mind before the boiling point. I feel like I try to please him and end up being taken for granted." She was learning that her feelings are appropriate and that she is justified in expressing them. She began to evolve as she distinguished between "being feelings" and "having feelings" and expressing them. The need for approval and to please became less important than recognizing her own needs and bringing them forth. The essential style of **Twos** is a cycle of pleasing others to win love. The method of accomplishing this goal is to merge with the other, knowing the other's needs more than one's own. Barbara's history reflects this conflict.

When she was a young child, Barbara's parents divorced. As in most cases, she remained in her mother's care, and as a **Two** merged totally with her mother. Barbara commented in a session, "I thought I would hurt my Mom if I wasn't just like her. Mom was vulnerable and emotional, but I don't like myself as an emotional person."

Barbara's first boyfriend was two years older, handsome, and in the fast crowd. As she reports, she was anxious to please him and please her parents because "It was time not to be a virgin and I wanted to prove that nothing was wrong with me." Barbara admits, "I was very confused. He told me he had herpes, but I didn't know the rules. I wanted to make him feel okay. I got herpes and felt betrayed."

In the last few years, Barbara L. has been in a feminist reading group. "I have at one point or another identified with each of them. I want others to accept me. I am lost in my confusion. I don't have a real self."

In the above examples, Barbara's struggle to claim her "real self" and have appropriate boundaries is evident. Increased awareness of her tendency to merge has allowed her to be less passive. She now has active choice in meeting the needs of others or not. Barbara continues to get more in touch with her own needs as well as expressing them. With the shift from needing less approval (external frame) toward inner knowing (internal frame), Barbara is beginning to claim her real self. Her dance has enhanced her confidence in her body, and this has significantly empowered her along her evolutionary path.

* * * * *

Mary F. is a 42-year-old married woman who sought treatment for anxiety and depression. She also complained of a number of somatic symptoms including palpitations, obesity, and irritable bowel syndrome. Initially she indicated that she was experiencing some marital difficulties, but when couples therapy was recommended she backed off and remained ambivalent about it.

Exploration of the marital conflict revealed a certain pattern: she became very angry at her husband whenever he did not behave toward their sons and toward his parents in the manner she thought proper; yet she was afraid that her anger would displease others. She felt that her husband did not love her if he didn't anticipate her needs and do what she wanted.

She became aware that she believed if she couldn't control her husband, he would become separate and different from her, which to her meant abandonment. This fear was another reason she couldn't stand up for herself, feeling that if she did, she would be unlovable. Her somatic symptoms were manifestations of her anger, fear, and helplessness. Further discussion of the marital relationship made it clear that she was reluctant to change anything in the relationship because it meant that she would have to change herself. She was invested in ensuring her family's happiness, and convinced that any change in her behavior would upset her perceived control of her family.

Exploration of her cognitive processes revealed a strong external frame of reference, a primary sort by people, a tendency to match, and virtually no awareness of visual or auditory experience. She even described herself as a "massive blob of feeling." In describing boundaries, she said, "Everyone has a piece of me . . . when my son goes away to school, it's like my heart is torn out of my chest, he takes a piece of me . . . when he goes away. There's nothing of me left." She experienced this viscerally, hence it was important to keep her sons and her husband close to her. When they rebelled against this constriction and control (which they described to her as being "manipulative and intrusive"), she felt devastated and abandoned. Her hurt and helplessness led them to feel even more controlled and manipulated.

THERAPEUTIC APPROACH FOR TWOS

Twos' fundamental strategy to deal with survival and safety is being loved. "When I'm loved, I'm safe." This strategy creates the tendency to lose boundaries, merge, and to be too dependent on others' opinions and values. The core issue for **Twos** is identity (Who am I?). **Twos'** basic defensive position is **toward** (acceptance and approval from others), and they come from the **heart** as their center of intelligence (thinking through their emotions). The traditional psychological diagnosis is hysteria and dependency. Translating into NLP terms, there is a lack of boundaries between thinking and emotions, and self and others; a lack of internal frame of reference and an overdeveloped kinesthetic emotional system. Therapeutically, **Twos** need guidance to develop an internal frame of reference (a strong sense of ego), to maintain appropriate boundaries in intimate and significant relationships, and to establish a strategy to say "no" and pursue with comfort what they want for themselves (instead of getting it through pleasing, manipulating, and loving others). They need to learn to think—to use their inner visual and auditory systems with choice, and to value these systems as much as they do their kinesthetic system. **Twos** need to appreciate their ability to be separate and be loved.

NLP PATTERNS
(See Appendix 1 for definitions)

Sort by People	Mind Read
Chunk Large	Associated
Kinesthetic Emotional	In Time
Match	External Frame of Reference
Attend to Other's Internal	Criteria: Acceptance &
State	Freedom

SPECIFIC NLP THERAPEUTIC INTERVENTIONS

As therapists we have found that the progress and evolution of our clients depend upon three categories of development: **Boundaries, Beliefs** and **Criteria**, and **Internal/External Worlds**. Since the Enneagram system is a dynamic one, the limitations and challenges of each personality type fall into issues relating to boundaries; to negative beliefs and conflicting and/or rigid criteria; and to a preoccupation with either the inner or the outer world which results in an imbalance and/or impaired relationship between the two. Therefore we have organized our interventions within these categories.

BOUNDARIES
• Develop Self/Other boundaries. Question the desire to please and the reluctance to say no. Intervene by using the **Boundary Model and Process** to enable **Twos** to have more choice about merging. The **Boundaries Process** will help them build boundaries when there are none and facilitate their evolution.
• Challenge the assumption that **Twos** always know what is best for those they care about, and that those they care about should know what they need and want. Use the **Perceptual Positions Process** and the **Changing Expectations Process**. These processes will help to challenge and transform **Twos'** tendency to manipulate for approval and love.

BELIEFS & CRITERIA
• Belief change work is necessary for **Twos**. The belief, "Others' needs and wants are more important than mine" is limiting and causes low self-esteem. Altered beliefs such as "My needs are just as important as another's;" "I can recognize and take care of my own needs and still be loved by another;" or "I can be separate and connected" give **Twos** a greater sense of self. To achieve this, use the **Reimprinting Process** and the **Submodality Belief Change Process**.
• Challenge the dichotomy of their criteria of acceptance and freedom. Suggest that it is possible to be separate, remain connected, and still be accepted. Come up with some **Counter Examples** of when that may have worked, or ask them to **Model**

other people who are accepted and still remain separate.

• The tendency to somaticize will decrease as **Twos** get in touch with the belief that they deserve to get what they need and want and can still be accepted. Anger will be less repressed as they learn to express and acknowledge their deep needs. The hysteria which causes the somatized condition will diminish. Being loved and accepted without manipulating will give **Twos** freedom and clear access to the inner truths that they know so well, and the path toward the highest evolution for a **Two**—unconditional love—is opened.

INTERNAL/EXTERNAL WORLDS

• Notice the difference between Self and Others. Do **Spacial Reframe** to integrate the different parts and make **Twos** comfortable with their own unique selves. This process can strengthen the internal frame of reference.

• Reinforce the internal frame of reference by developing submodality exercises to strengthen the auditory and visual systems.

• Teach them to chunk down and question their own mind reading. Encourage them to actually check out their mind reading and find out how chunking down and being more specific gives them more useful information. This awareness will give them the choice to sort by information as well as by people.

• Teach them to mismatch; give tasks to develop ability to mismatch others' posture and breathing, and notice how they are different from others as well as similar.

• Use **Reclaim Personal History Process** to enhance and support inner resources and build a stronger internal frame of reference.

THREE: THE DOER-ACHIEVER

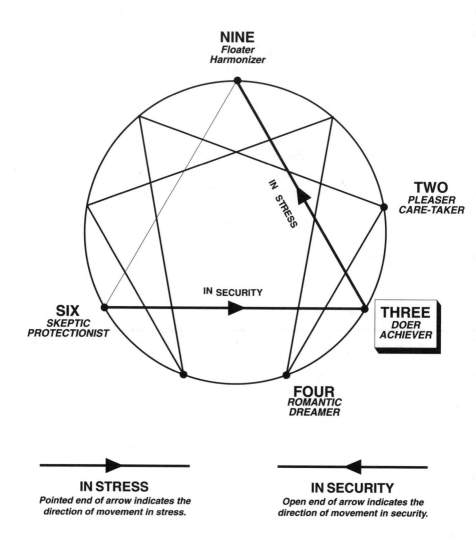

IN STRESS
Pointed end of arrow indicates the direction of movement in stress.

IN SECURITY
Open end of arrow indicates the direction of movement in security.

NOTE: The way that each individual defines and gives meaning to the words Stress and Security is idiosyncratic. Stress is not necessarily experienced as negative and security is not necessarily experienced as positive.

Chapter 5

THREE: THE DOER-ACHIEVER

Threes are the Doer-Achievers. Their wing is either the Pleaser-Caretaker (Two) or the Romantic-Dreamer (Four). In stress, they move to the Floater-Harmonizer (Nine) and in security to the Skeptic-Protectionist (Six).**Threes** are chiefly concerned with success and achievement and avoid any sense of failure. Their main defense is deceit of the essential self; their main issue is identity (Who am I?) since their identity is often tightly bound up with what they do. Their intelligence is centered in the heart, and their most comfortable style of being is doing.

Main Filter or Focus of Attention: External approval of what they do/accomplish.

Childhood Theme/Concern: Threes were rewarded and given attention and praise for their achievements. Performance or image was valued rather than emotional connections or involvement with people. Winning and being number one is extremely important. Emphasis on competition and conformity to acceptable images is strong.

Personality Traits: Threes have a strong drive toward accomplishment and success; they are goal-oriented. They are popular, persuasive, self-confident, have a positive attitude; they are busy, efficient, good promoters, aggressive and energetic, and are socially skilled. They are excellent at planning the future. The appearance of success is of primary importance to **Threes** as they are very status-conscious and aware of the image they create. They may look for a mate to complete the image. They are competitive, have a fast tempo, and like to be the center of attention. **Threes** often create busy work just to keep any feelings of inadequacy under control. Expecting to feel loved for what they do and what they accomplish rather than who they are, they hide what they truly feel and think. As their security depends on how much they do, they often confuse their real self with their job. They use excessive activity to avoid intimacy, even becoming workaholics, with many exhibiting polyphasic behaviors—doing two or more things at once. They control through activity and are secretly afraid of being seen as a phony and then being rejected. At work, they are good decision-makers and tend to be successful. Since work is of utmost importance, relationships are secondary and real intimacy difficult; paradoxically **Threes** seem to need to keep a love interest around, but distanced.

Typical Beliefs: Worth depends on achievement. I am what I do. I must produce to be loved.

Typical Compelling Question: "What do I have to do to succeed?" "Am I successful?" "Am I getting across?" "Is what I'm doing a success? Is it being noticed? approved?"

Boundary Issues: Walls exist between body and emotions, between self and others. Walls between true and false selves and the present and future. Intimacy can lead to a loss of boundaries between self and the significant other.

Attention Shifts for Personal Evolution: Evolution for **Threes** depends upon their creating boundaries between body and emotions, slowing down in order to develop their inner world and connecting with their own internal values and emotions. These attention shifts enable them to develop more of an internal frame of reference and separate their identity from what they accomplish.

Specifics: **Threes** should sort by people, become more receptive (passive) and present-oriented. Develop the kinesthetic emotional system—allow emotions to rise to consciousness and connect to them. Stay with and witness uncomfortable emotions instead of "doing" something else. Develop and appreciate inner observer part. **Threes** need to pay attention to the impact their behavior has on others' emotions. Change the belief, "I am what I do."

VIGNETTES

Betsey Wright, a long-time close aide to Bill Clinton said about him, "I can see that he doesn't believe that he, as a person, is worthy of being liked, but that he has these accomplishments that will make people want to like him and make him worth liking."

* * * * *

During a seminar in Brussels on the Enneagram, after everyone had had his/her type identified, the teacher asked people to form groups of the same type and eat lunch together. It was summer and everyone ate outside on the lawn. More than 80 people were present; each type had at least eight representatives. As the teacher visited each group, she noticed that she could not find the **Threes**. There **was** a circle of personal items—notebooks, pens, cases, scarves, glasses—as though 10 people had been there, had marked their places, and would return. The teacher asked where the **Threes** were and was told that they had all had gone off to look after business! Very typical of **Threes**: they never stay put if they can help it.

* * * * *

Beatrice spoke of a dear friend with whom she also had a professional relationship. Having met through work, their first interactions were work-related, and since they both worked at a fast tempo they got along famously. As the friendship developed, they decided to spend more personal time together and go away every year for three or four days. But the first time they did this, Beatrice said her friend drove her crazy! Beatrice slowed down considerably on vacation; her friend did not. Beatrice realized that her friend's fast tempo was disturbing her, and that her friend was a **Three**. She was then able to make adjustments and shift her expectations. Eventually Beatrice got her friend to begin to evolve on the time and activity front and have some choice about slowing down her tempo, depending on the circumstances and context.

CASE HISTORIES

Kurt M., a business man, is occupied with "doing" or "performing" in order to maintain a certain image. (Activity and producing ideas allow **Threes** to stay removed from real emotions.) It is almost impossible for Kurt M. to deal directly with situations involving emotions or unpleasant confrontation. He arrived in my office because of his wife, who had been contemplating a divorce for a long time. She reported that when she confronted her husband with the possible dissolution of their marriage, he acted as if he hadn't heard her and directed the discussion to other topics—their children and how wonderful they were, or the new house they had just completed in Long Island. These diversions insured that Kurt M. "looked good" and could avoid the heart of the matter.

Threes fall into image. As children, they find safety in image and achievement. Kurt M. is good looking, socially well-connected, business wise, and he spends a lot of time smiling and hand shaking. He works for a prestigious Wall Street firm. In most of our sessions, he has an eye on future goals. These goals very rarely pinpoint any marital difficulties and focus more on his career and how to succeed in business. The challenge in therapy was to get him to confront the truth of his situation and access the hidden emotions generated by the problems at home.

In an attempt to identify even the most rudimentary feelings, I asked if he had had a good time on his vacation. Kurt M. commented, "If I hadn't gone on this golfing trip in the Bahamas sponsored by the Country Club, my name would have been taken off THE list." Seeking approval and being on THE list are the criteria; having a good time or feeling good about the vacation weren't considered.

Like many politicians, **Threes** have difficulty sorting out the difference between their inner self and what they do. "I am what

I do" is the unconscious belief driving their behavior. The wall between the real self and the performer/achiever self blocks awareness, and inner growth is slow and sometimes impossible. If the outer shell cracks and the image is tarnished, safety is threatened.

* * * * *

Pam W. is a **Three** whose shell cracked slightly in a therapy session when she revealed a traumatic and failed romance. Prior to her marriage, Pam W. was deeply in love and ultimately was rejected, which is a great threat to a **Three**. Ordinarily, this client has very little grounded weight in her body. She is dissociated from her body and speaks as if she is measuring how her words will sound, listening and floating from above. When Pam W. talked of this failed relationship, her body became heavy, and her voice gushed forth with words filled with pain.

In a culture that is only beginning to encourage male expressions of emotion, male **Threes** such as Kurt M. have great difficulty taking down the wall between the self and emotions on the path to fuller evolution. Female **Threes** such as Pam W. have a somewhat easier time. Massage therapy in coordination with psychotherapy is a powerful intervention. Since America is a **Three** culture that rewards winning, status, and success, it is very difficult for a **Three** to evolve. The culture rewards **Threes** for not evolving.

THERAPEUTIC APPROACH FOR THREES

Threes' fundamental strategy for survival and safety is to achieve and achieve. "If I succeed I'm safe." This strategy results in excessive doing, numerous activities, and emphasis on the external world; image and status become disproportionately important. For **Threes**, the core issue is identity (Who am I?). Their basic defensive position is **toward** approval for achieving, and their center of intelligence is the **heart**—using emotions to fulfill self-image, i.e. giving to others to look good. They are seldom in touch with their emotions and avoid real emotional gratification; within traditional psychological diagnosis, **Threes**

are considered workaholics, or Type A personalities. Translated into NLP terms, they favor activity, doing, external behavior and world, while neglecting emotions and their inner world.

Therapeutically, **Threes** need guidance to develop a stronger internal frame of reference, to separate essence from what they accomplish, to transform the belief "I am what I do," and to slow down. It is crucial for them to establish permeable boundaries between their external and internal worlds, and between their activities and emotions. They need to learn to value their inner world so that they achieve more balance with their obsessive doing. Therapists must be careful not to allow **Threes** to turn therapy into a project to be accomplished, rather than using therapy to learn to be comfortable and to feel worthwhile simply in **being**. It is important for **Threes** to make a real commitment to the therapeutic process and relationship.

NLP PATTERNS
(see Appendix 1 for definitions)

Pro-active	Subordinate Present for Future
Self-oriented	Fast Tempo
Kinesthetic Primary & Visual	External Frame of Reference
Sort by Activity	Modal Operator: "I want"
Towards	External Behavior of Self and
Future-oriented	Others
	Dissociate from Body
	Criteria: Accomplishments
	& Looking Good

SPECIFIC NLP THERAPEUTIC INTERVENTIONS

As therapists we have found that the progress and evolution of our clients depend upon three categories of development: Boundaries, Beliefs and Criteria, and Internal/External Worlds. Since the Enneagram system is a dynamic one, the limitations and challenges of each personality type fall into issues relating to boundaries; to negative beliefs and conflicting and/or rigid criteria; and to a preoccupation with either the inner or the outer world which results in an imbalance and/or impaired relationship between the two. Therefore we have organized our interventions within these categories.

BOUNDARIES
• Utilize the **Change History Process** to have **Threes** shift past memories so that they can feel good about themselves even when they did not produce or accomplish. This process will add value to their inner world and reinforce a stronger internal frame of reference.
• Use the **Boundary Model and Process** to build permeable boundaries between the body and the emotions. Allow the emotions to rise to the conscious mind, locate them in the body, connect to them and express them; thus developing the emotional kinesthetic system. Through boundary work, assist **Threes** to be more in the present by allowing information and emotions to flow between past, present, and future.

BELIEFS & CRITERIA
• Change belief, "I am what I do/what I achieve" to a belief that includes the value of being. Use the **Reimprinting Process** to separate essence from behavior. Use **Reframe (6-step)** to find the positive intention/function beneath doing and accomplishing to establish other choices.

INTERNAL/EXTERNAL WORLDS
• Encourage personal evolution as an important criterion; this criterion is in direct opposition to just looking good. Help **Threes** experience **being** rather than **doing** in order to feel worthwhile. Use **Spacial Reframe, Submodality Processes** and tasks to slow clients down in order to facilitate this.
• Teach **Threes** to slow down and find value in doing less. This intervention will help them stay with and witness uncomfortable emotions instead of **doing** something else. Have **Threes** notice **what** they do to avoid feeling. Make them aware of their need to fulfill an image which keeps them doing and away from feelings.
• Use **Reclaim Personal History Process** to strengthen inner resources and support an internal frame of reference.
• Give **Threes** exercises to sort by other and to become less self-

absorbed. Challenge them, using their criterion of accomplishment, to shift attention to the impact their behavior has on others. Give them tasks to pay attention to others' emotions.

• Task them to change their posture from upright and slightly leaning forward to leaning back. This will support the choice to be less active and more passive (receptive).

FOUR: THE ROMANTIC-DREAMER

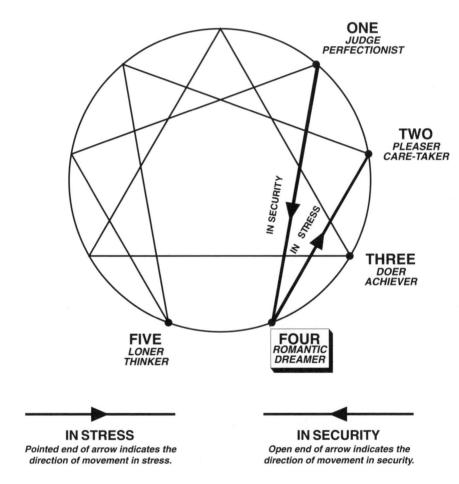

IN STRESS
*Pointed end of arrow indicates the
direction of movement in stress.*

IN SECURITY
*Open end of arrow indicates the
direction of movement in security.*

NOTE: The way that each individual defines and gives meaning
to the words Stress and Security is idiosyncratic. Stress
is not necessarily experienced as negative and security is
not necessarily experienced as positive.

Chapter 6

FOUR: THE ROMANTIC-DREAMER

Fours are the Romantic-Dreamers. Their wing is either the Doer-Achiever (Three) or the Loner-Thinker (Five). In stress they move to the Pleaser-Caretaker (Two) and in security to the Judge-Perfectionist (One). They are chiefly concerned with being special/unique and avoid at all costs being ordinary. They alternate between melancholy and elated gaiety. Their primary defense is envy and their fundamental issue is identity (Who am I?), with an almost compulsive and unrelenting concern with themselves and who they are. Their intelligence is centered in the heart. Their most comfortable style of being is feeling.

Main Filter or Focus of Attention: The best in what's absent and the worst in what's present.

Childhood Theme/Concern: **Fours** have a sense of abandonment, loss and deprivation—sometimes with physical or psychological abuse. Often their mothers seem omnipotent, competitive and narcissistic. Sometimes a **Four** is born into a family where the child is valued for identification with the pain of one or the other parent.

Personality Traits: **Fours** have a strong inclination toward the creative, artistic and romantic. They are sensitive, committed to beauty, sex, intensity, death and melancholy. Very emotional, they tend to dramatize their emotions. They are often lonely souls in search of beauty and longing for the beloved. Their external presentation is dramatic—they often wear blacks and purples. They have a fundamental need to be special, unique, with a strong sense of entitlement; they abhor being ordinary. They are crisis-oriented, attention-grabbers. They experience emotional highs and lows which result in swings from anguish, shame, and hurt to excessive energy, gregariousness and concentrated periods of arduous work. **Fours** are attracted to edge-of-life experiences; these can be psychological or physical, e.g., risky driving, fast cars and roller coasters. They are attracted to the tragic and to the unattainable and are very aware of what they don't have—what's missing in their life. They have a tendency to reject before being rejected. Their belief that others have what they lack leads them in to the trap of envy. Intensive self-other comparisons make **Fours** very competitive. They may have a tendency toward suffering, depression, regret, and self-criticism—sometimes with an internal sense of shame. They are self-absorbed and narcissistic; they daydream and have trouble completing projects. Often **Fours** are burdened with a distorted body-image; this sometimes leads to anorexia and/or bulimia. While consciously wishing for gratification, they unconsciously move away from or reject it; e.g., they move away from abandonment yet avoid love and intimacy by noticing how their partner never lives up to their standards. They tend not to be good with groups, are better one on one, and can be very helpful to others who suffer. They can be good therapists and teachers.

Typical Beliefs: I'm missing out. There's always more/better. I'm not worthy of being loved. A special love will make me real/whole/complete/worthy. Others are getting what I want. If I get what others have, I'll find my authentic self. I have to be special/unique.

Typical Compelling Question: "How can I be loved?" "Am I being loved enough?" "Am I the way I need to be?" "Who loves me?" "What do you think of me?" "Do you notice me?"

Boundary Issues: Lack of Internal/External, Self/Other Boundaries.

Attention Shifts for Personal Evolution: Evolution for **Fours** comes with the choice to appreciate self and others without envy; to notice what they already have and can do, letting go of "if onlys" and extreme idealization. By paying more attention to and giving more value to their external world, they will achieve more of a balance between their inner and outer worlds. The development of boundaries between these worlds, and between self and other, will help **Fours** modify their habitual internal self-criticism.

Specifics: **Fours** need to develop more choices and control in their auditory system. Learn to match congruently. Become more pro-active, toward, and other-oriented. Live more in the present; check out external reality more. Recognize difference between real and idealized emotions. Transform envy into motivation to learn and change. Develop real internal frame of reference. Witness and modify internal critical voice. Direct more positive attention toward the external world and the choice to be in **Uptime**.

VIGNETTES

At a conference for female doctors using alternative medical approaches, I overheard a conversation in which a woman in her 40s was talking about her health problems. Apparently she was diabetic and suffered from numerous allergies and other ailments. Every time someone would mention possible therapeutic approaches, she replied that she had already tried this or that—and it didn't work. Finally she said, "These things work for many of my patients, I'm just different—at least I'm special!" This woman was dressed stunningly all in black and ate celery and carrot sticks throughout the conference.

* * * * *

Constance was thoroughly upset with her friend Betty. When Constance was in a crisis, Betty was attentive and sympathetic, but whenever things were going well for Constance, Betty never seemed interested. Once when Constance was describing several positive situations in her professional life, Betty deliberately changed the subject and began to talk continuously about what was going well in her life—never even bothering to comment or reply to what Constance had been saying. Another time when Constance had been reporting about a success she had had, Betty interrupted and told her, "I really must tell you I cannot feel good about what you're telling me—I feel envious and just bad . . . ."

Having realized that Betty is a **Four** and not very evolved in the area of friendship, Constance has to decide whether it is worth it to her to continue the friendship and to modify her expectations. If Constance decides to continue the friendship, this realization will allow her to appreciate Betty's other positive qualities and not be so hurt and disturbed by her selfishness.

* * * * *

Berta Y., a participant in a seminar, described how at ten she was a star. Then she went from an alternative to a traditional school and, as she said, was crushed. In her new school she was no longer a star; she just wasn't unique any more. Berta Y. commented that she was experiencing the seminar in the same way. She considered herself a star, a workshop leader, and an author. Yet, as a student at this particular seminar, with a leader who was a charismatic and dynamic woman close to her own age, Berta Y. complained that she was no longer special. "I think I should avoid any situation in which I do not experience myself as a star."

CASE HISTORIES

Gail L. is a poet whose life revolves around her feelings— feelings about her art, feelings about significant others and feelings of empathy toward humanity. To earn a living she does house painting. At this point in time, she is painting John Lennon's son's apartment. In our last therapy session she was consumed with grief and burst into tears, exclaiming, "What a waste—John's killing was such a waste." Gail L. can swing from gushing tears to uproarious laughter. This manic behavior is part of the **Fours'** style of being. This behavior is accompanied with a melancholia that is sweet and almost delicious. The following is one of Gail L.'s poems:

> Oh Melancholia
> served for drink in spring
> oh, melancholia
> this humor fluid through the corpus
> this black bile
> made sweet through distillation
> from bitter refinement
> drop by drop.
> Oh, melancholia
> served for drink in spring
> oh, melancholia
> to wet my lips and drown
> but not drink.
> The swill left
> we graze beyond the waste of the homo sapiens.
> Night to sleep
> drown in tidal waves of syrup sweet
> sweet dreams.
> Melancholia.

Gail L.'s work in therapy has given her more awareness and allowed her to claim more of her power. On days when evidence of her slow but steady evolution is clear, she is less indulgent about her feelings; less whiny, less stuck in nostalgia, and less reckless. **Fours** who are less evolved are often reckless and may become victims. Some years earlier, Gail L. often exhibited extremely reckless behavior. Once she found herself in a precarious situation, late at night, with a merchant in the East Village who raped her. She subsequently exercised her power—and took him to court, winning the case. Recklessness and dauntlessness in the **Four** often lead to victim situations and crises. Many therapists, myself included, find the crisis cycle to be a common theme with many **Fours**. This style can have numerous manifestations—from crazy taxi rides, through to chronic joblessness to homes burning to the ground. The high level of excitement of the "on the edge" crisis is almost like an addiction and always ensures the depressive swing down to sweet melancholia.

In the less-evolved **Four**, there is little balance between the internal and external reference frame. Association is to the inner life of feeling. When **Fours** look to the outside and compare themselves to others, something is most often missing. Their lives don't match up; the other person always has it better, the grass is greener.

Among **Fours**, envy is a common emotion. In any relationship to a significant other, a **Four** is preoccupied with how it isn't working or, again, what is missing. One day in session, Gail L. exclaimed, "I can't stand living with my lover any more. She is too filthy and messy. I'm just leaving." This lack of contentment and tendency to polarize keeps a **Four** on the edge, recycling into crisis. When Gail L. won second prize in a poetry contest, she blurted out, "**If only** it had been first prize. I'm going to give up writing and go back to the time when I was free of all this." In reaction, Gail L. polarized from winning to not writing at all, to returning to the nostalgia of the past. In pain **Fours** retreat toward the seductive memories of the past.

* * * * *

Agnes C. is a 48-year-old married woman who, after three and a half years of intensive individual and group therapy, came in and reported that **for the first time** things were going well and she didn't have anything negative to deal with. This state of affairs actually made her fairly nervous. "Perhaps there was no point in being alive if there was nothing negative to overcome." In the past she had stated that normality and stability were totally boring and uninteresting and made her seem like everyone else.

Agnes C.'s presentation is striking—she is flamboyant in appearance and gesture, and her speech has overtones of Shakespearean oratory and rhetoric. She is quite bright and well-educated in the classics and humanities (she despises having a mundane career as an accountant), and seeks to use the most complex vocabulary and grammatical constructs that she possibly can. However, she systematically undermines her own creative and literary inclinations; a tendency rooted in extraordinarily intense and deep-seated reciprocal envy between her and her mother. She firmly but angrily believes that her mother can be the only artist in the family. Agnes C. has spent her life grieving the loss of the good mothering that she never had, the satisfying marriage she never had (she's been married twice), the children she never had (she has one son who is a successful professional in his own field), and her own potential that she never manifested.

Her affect is stormy, and moods rigidly move from high to low and back again. She believes that she embodies the essence of depression and has elevated suffering and loss to an art. She can give the impression of arrogance, particularly with her style of speech, but inside there is a profound sense of shame and self-loathing, which is compounded by a problem with compulsive eating and obesity. This shame and self-loathing make her hypersensitive to the slightest potential for abandonment and rejection, which she feels is a central dynamic in her relationship with her mother.

THERAPEUTIC APPROACH FOR FOURS

Fours' fundamental strategy for survival and safety is their indulgence in melancholy. "If I suffer I'm safe." This strategy results in overdramatization of emotions, narcissistic self-absorption, and an overriding sense of regret and envy. Their core issue is identity (Who am I?). **Fours'** basic defensive position is **toward** approval and acceptance **from** self, and their center of intelligence is the **heart**, in that they **are** their emotions. The traditional, psychological diagnosis is depressive, bi-polar disorders. Described in NLP terms, their primary awareness and value is concentrated on their own internal state, emotions, with excessive mind reading, mismatching, and a lack of a true internal frame of reference. Therapeutically, **Fours** need to establish more of a balance between the value they place on the internal and external worlds; they need to develop a stronger internal frame of reference, learn to match themselves (i.e., notice and appreciate what they already have and can do), maintain healthy bound-aries and let go of the obsessive need always to be special/unique. **Fours** often gravitate toward more traditional psychoanalysis because of the attention and drama and because actual change is not necessarily an important goal. While this form of therapy can be useful to some individuals, it may be counterproductive for a **Four**.

NLP PATTERNS
(see Appendix 1 for definitions)

Mismatch
Polarize
Away
Kinesthetic/Emotional
Compare Self to Others
External Frame of Reference
Passive

In Time
Past-oriented
Universal Quantifiers
Model Operator: "should
    have been"
Downtime
Self-oriented
Criteria: Being Unique
    & Being Authentic

SPECIFIC NLP THERAPEUTIC INTERVENTIONS

As therapists we have found that the progress and evolution of our clients depends upon three categories of development: **Boundaries, Beliefs** and **Criteria,** and **Internal/External Worlds.** Since the Enneagram system is a dynamic one, the limitations and challenges of each personality type fall into issues relating to boundaries; to negative beliefs and conflicting and/or rigid criteria; and to a preoccupation with either the inner or the outer world which results in an imbalance and/or impaired relationship between the two. Therefore we have organized our interventions within these categories.

BOUNDARIES
• Use **Boundary Model and Process** to assist **Fours** to achieve a balance between their internal and external worlds. Teach them how to get into the observer-self (2nd position), using the **Per-**

ceptual Positions Process. This self-awareness will assist them to monitor their swings from hyperactivity/joy to solitude/melancholia.

• Use the **Change History Process** to shift and transform painful memories into resources, especially since **Fours'** painful memories tend to be without boundaries and permeate their existence.

• Help **Fours** recognize the difference between real and idealized emotions as well as their tendency to compare themselves to the idealized other (the envied one)—and to recognize envy as an emotion to learn from and not stay stuck in. Use envy as motivation. Use the **Perceptual Positions Process** and the **Self-to-Other Comparison** Process on real and imagined interactions that result in envy.

BELIEFS & CRITERIA

• Criteria work is useful in dealing with the issue of being special/unique. Challenge the idea that true authenticity really exists only with those people who behave as if they are always special/unique. Since "being special/unique" and finding "authenticity" are important to **Fours**, it may not be possible to have both. Utilize **Criteria Ladder**, and **Adjusting the Complex Equivalence** for being special/unique and authentic.

• Use the **Reimprinting Process** to change beliefs such as, "Others are getting what I want," "A special love will make me complete and whole," "I have to be special/unique."

INTERNAL/EXTERNAL WORLDS

• Be clear with the **Four** that therapy work is for change and evolution, and that it is not just another method of getting attention and drama. Use the **Smart Outcome Model** to create a satisfactory contract.

• Challenge **Fours'** need to be **special/unique** around the issue of suffering and pain. The sweet pain of melancholia can be a resource toward creativity but should not be an end in itself. It is important for **Fours** to feel special because they exist. Use **Reframing** (6-Step or Spacial if there is an inner conflict) with the part in charge of being special.

• Increase **Fours'** satisfaction with self by noticing what is there that is positive rather than what is missing. This realization will assist **Fours** to have the choice to match. This choice will prove more beneficial to self-esteem.

• Have **Fours** witness and modify their internal critical voice and develop more choice in the auditory system. **Submodality** work is effective for this change.

• Through **Time Line** work, reorient **Fours** from the past, from regrets and from "if onlys" **to** the present and the future.

• Use **Reclaim Personal History** to strengthen experience of inner resources and internal frame of reference.

• Teach **Fours** to recognize depression as a signal about some change they need to make in their life and use it as a reminder (trigger) to do something in the external world. Emphasize the need to take action, get into **Uptime**, and pay attention to others rather than self.

FIVE: THE LONER-THINKER

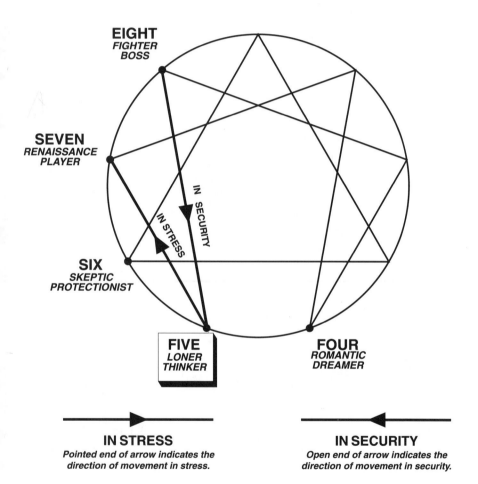

IN STRESS
Pointed end of arrow indicates the direction of movement in stress.

IN SECURITY
Open end of arrow indicates the direction of movement in security.

NOTE: The way that each individual defines and gives meaning to the words Stress and Security is idiosyncratic. Stress is not necessarily experienced as negative and security is not necessarily experienced as positive.

Chapter 7

FIVE: THE LONER-THINKER

Fives are the Loner-Thinkers. Their wing is either the Romantic-Dreamer (Four) or the Skeptic-Protectionist (Six). In stress they move to the Renaissance-Player (Seven) and in security to the Fighter-Boss (Eight). They are chiefly concerned with the accumulation of knowledge. They avoid stupidity and social involvement through isolation and avoid a sense of emptiness through thinking. Their primary defenses are isolation, analyzing, and formulating. Their fundamental issue is fear—fear of involvement and emotions. They are stingy with their emotions, giving only a part of themselves and compartmentalizing their life. Their most comfortable style of being is thinking, and their center of intelligence is the head.

Main Filter or Focus of Attention: What others want from them.

Main Childhood Theme/Concern: Family was experienced as very intrusive so that the child closed down emotionally in order to get away. Some form of withdrawal on the part of the child is central. Having experienced not being wanted—being left alone became synonymous with safety. Abandonment was handled by detachment of feelings.

Personality Traits: Fives are intellectual, logical, original thinkers, patient, self-sufficient, independent, knowledgeable. They are more comfortable with mental pursuits—thinking rather than feeling, and one could say, almost addicted to knowledge. They covet their privacy and need a lot of space and time to self. They tend to compartmentalize their lives and experience their emotions more easily when alone than with others. **Fives** dislike working with others and have trouble with authority figures, fearful of being threatened or overwhelmed. They are critical, afraid of emotions, and will withdraw rather than confront; they can be drained or upset by others' expectations. There is a tendency to settle for less and become isolated—a hermit. They pull back from the outside world, even from their bodies (kinesthetic consciousness), hoarding their energy. They avoid competition and will withdraw attention from strong emotions, focusing on information instead. Facts and information are more important than action. **Fives** can have trouble doing and accomplishing anything concrete in the world. Often they are not socially-skilled. Although **Fives** are fearful of emotions, once they trust you and allow you into their space, they display strong emotions. Under stress **Fives** have access to anger and uncontrolled rage.

Typical Beliefs: You can only rely on self. Knowledge and analyzing is safety. The mind and thinking are the highest values. You can't trust emotions. Logic is most important.

Typical Compelling Question: "How does this work?" "Do I know enough?"

Boundary Issues: Fives put walls around different areas of life—contextual walls, and around feelings, head, heart and body. In intimate relationships, however, they tend to lose boundaries completely.

Attention Shifts for Personal Evolution: Evolution for **Fives** comes with more balance between thinking and feeling. They must challenge their own tendencies to withdraw and should stay connected to their emotions and to those of others. It is important for **Fives** to ask for more of what they want emotionally. Creating boundaries instead of walls and making friends of their emotions will contribute significantly to the evolution and development of **Fives**.

Specifics: Fives must develop both their kinesthetic emotional and kinesthetic primary systems. They must learn to be comfortable with emotions and the expression of emotions. They should become more pro-active, initiating and completing projects. They should acquire the choice to be associated. They should challenge values of secrecy, superiority, and separateness, and sort more by activity and people. To evolve, **Fives** need to become more externally-oriented and other-oriented.

VIGNETTES

Taken from **Journal of a Solitude**, by May Sarton:
"On the mantel, in the Japanese jar, two sprays of white lilies, recurved, maroon pollen on the stamens, and a branch of peony leaves turned a strange pinkish brown . . . When I am alone the flowers are really seen; I can pay attention to them. They are felt as presences . . . . For a long time now, every meeting with another human being has been a collision. I feel too much, sense too much, am exhausted by the reverberations after even the simplest conversation. . . . It may be outwardly silent here but in the back of my mind is a clamor of human voices, too many needs, hopes, fears. . . . I often feel exhausted, but it is not my work that tires (work is a rest); it is the effort of pushing away the lives and needs of others before I can come to the work with any freshness and zest."

* * * * *

Lucille was troubled by James, her oldest son, who lived in Chicago. When in Chicago, he did not call or write or have much contact with the rest of his family who lived in Toronto. When a member of the family did reach him by phone, or when he visited (which was two or three times a year for extended periods of time), he was warm, lively, interested in what the other was doing, and very concerned about the welfare of his family. Lucille knew that James was very connected to the family, but when he left to go back to his home, he seemed to drop off the face of the earth. It was very confusing and seemed extremely contradictory. However, James is a **Five**. He compartmentalizes his life, putting walls around different areas, different contexts. Hence, when he is with his family he's totally there, close and caring. When he leaves to return home to Chicago, a different area and context of his life, he walls off and compartmentalizes his family. He cares about his family, but when he isn't in that context, they get put away in a different compartment. James has a problem: he hasn't yet learned to transform the walls into permeable boundaries. When Lucille realized that her son was a **Five**, his behavior made sense and she stopped taking it so personally. Of course, she's hoping that he will evolve more and become aware of his shortcomings in this area!

CASE HISTORIES

Peter G. takes a position on the outside of life, observing and gathering information. He often comments on how difficult it was to join in at parties and festivities of any sort. He is much more comfortable on the side lines, drinking one or two beers, outside the action and laughter of others.

Peter G. is a good looking, bright man who has held the same job in publishing for over twenty years. The work environment he has chosen is a safe one: all his colleagues keep their emotions in check. Complaints about work are repressed or minimally expressed. The atmosphere is one of a happy family that presents an image of satisfaction. Getting fired is almost impossible.

A typical **Five**, Peter G. detaches in times of personal conflict and avoids, if possible, any emotional interaction. In one therapy session, he admitted he was unable to tell the cleaning lady that she was overpolishing one of his hand-hewn sculptures, thereby ruining it. In another incident, his tenant was a suspect in the theft of Peter G.'s family heirloom candlesticks. On neither occasion did Peter G. feel able to confront the person. As he comments, "I felt safer not getting involved."

Peter G. has his own high standards of achievement and is guided by his strong internal frame of reference. From year to year he charts his own progress as a painter and sculptor. He is an artist part-time and is completely self-taught. Once Peter G. brought a series of self-portraits with him when he came to therapy. Remaining dissociated, he succinctly critiqued each one. Our therapy work concentrates on his essential being. Once he commented, "I never reveal the total me to anyone. I show different parts, depending upon the circumstances and who I am with." As the therapy continues, Peter G. strives toward feeling safe and being involved, participating and connecting with others emotionally and allowing his true feelings to emerge and be expressed appropriately.

* * * * *

Ellen F., a client, has a lover, Jim, who is an Observer (a **Five**). Ellen is a **Nine** and is often frustrated by Jim's tendency to keep her in the "relationship" compartment of his life rather than including her in his work life and in certain aspects of his leisure life. Jim is productive in his work life, but uses work to avoid feelings and intimacy and to maintain the walls between the contexts of his life.

Ellen reported that it took a very long time before they were able to reach a deep level of intimacy and trust (Jim has a strong Six wing), but that when that was achieved he became—and has remained—deeply loyal and affectionate. Jim has also become very open with her about issues and feelings that no one else has ever known about.

Knowledge, understanding, intelligence, and logical analysis are key values and skills for Jim, and he has no use for anyone who cannot or does not manifest these attributes. Ellen's ability to match and keep pace with his intellectual prowess formed the basis of the initial connection. Later, her skills with feeling and her perceptive sensitivity to his inner state opened some doors for him in the interpersonal arena and helped Jim learn about himself. As a result of their relationship, Jim can experience more and relate to his emotions rather than treating them as something unreliable, to be dissected and understood. He remains very guarded and cautious about the people and activities he becomes involved with and still will not take risks with anything he doesn't thoroughly understand.

THERAPEUTIC APPROACH FOR FIVES

Fives' fundamental strategy for survival and safety is their reliance on their mind and knowledge. "If I know enough I'll be safe." This strategy results in a severe imbalance between thinking and feeling, a walling-off of the emotions and withdrawal from others into solitude. Their core issue is **fear**. **Fives'** basic defensive position is **away** from involvement, and they come from the **head** as the center of their intelligence—thinking for the sake of thinking. The traditional psychological diagnosis is schizoid and avoidance. Described into NLP terms, **Fives** are dissociated, especially from their emotions and body; oriented toward self, information, and internal processes with little access to internal state (emotions) and little awareness of external behavior. Therapeutically, **Fives** need guidance to develop boundaries between their head, emotions, body, and the different contexts of their life, to learn to recognize and appreciate their emotions, and attend to what they want for themselves. **Fives** benefit greatly by developing the belief that they deserve to get what they want, and by learning to value people and emotions almost as much as information.

NLP PATTERNS
(see Appendix 1 for definitions)

Dissociated	Passive
Self-oriented	Lost Performatives
Internal Frame of Reference	Auditory
Sort by Information	Self & Other Internal Processes
Chunk Small	Criteria: Knowledge
	and Solitude

SPECIFIC NLP THERAPEUTIC INTERVENTIONS

As therapists we have found that the progress and evolution of our clients depends upon three categories of development: Boundaries, Beliefs and Criteria, and Internal/External Worlds. Since the Enneagram system is a dynamic one, the limitations and challenges of each personality type fall into issues relating to boundaries; to negative beliefs and conflicting and/or rigid criteria; and to a preoccupation with either the inner or the outer world which results in an imbalance and/or impaired relationship between the two. Therefore we have organized our interventions within these categories.

BOUNDARIES
• Utilize **Boundaries Model and Process** to help transform **Fives'** walls into permeable boundaries, allowing more connection with people, and less compartmentalization of their lives.

• Utilize the **Perceptual Positions Process** to enable **Fives** to identify and empathize with others and to get in touch with their own emotions while interacting with people.

BELIEFS & CRITERIA
• Identify the beliefs that foster fear of emotions. Use belief change methods: The **Submodality Process, Belief Change** and the **Reimprinting Process**.

• Use **Criteria Spin** to get **Fives** to value emotions as information for true knowledge and expand the Complex Equivalence of this value.

• Challenge and adjust the belief "knowledge makes you safe" by using the **Reimprinting Process**.

INTERNAL/EXTERNAL WORLDS
• Use **Reclaim Personal History** to reinforce emotions as a resource.

• **Model** someone who does trust his emotions.

• Use **Spacial Reframe** to create recognition and communication between parts that tend to be in conflict regarding withdrawal, emotions and connecting to people.

• Use the **Smart Outcome Model** to help **Fives** to develop their outcomes—establishing achievable goals makes them more conscious of what they want.

• Exercise such as swimming, walking and running awakens the kinesthetic primary system, which supports and reclaims body consciousness.

SIX: THE SKEPTIC-PROTECTIONIST

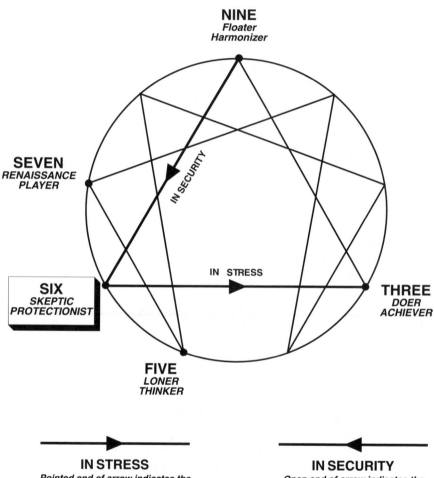

IN STRESS
*Pointed end of arrow indicates the
direction of movement in stress.*

IN SECURITY
*Open end of arrow indicates the
direction of movement in security.*

**NOTE: The way that each individual defines and gives meaning
to the words Stress and Security is idiosyncratic. Stress
is not necessarily experienced as negative and security is
not necessarily experienced as positive.**

Chapter 8

SIX: THE SKEPTIC-PROTECTIONIST

Sixes are the Skeptic-Protectionists. Their wing is either the Loner-Thinker (Five) or the Renaissance-Player (Seven). In stress they move to the Doer-Achiever (Three) and in security to the Floater-Harmonizer (Nine). They are chiefly concerned with security and authority. They avoid exposure—**Sixes** are more comfortable when invisible in some way. Their primary defense is self-doubt and projection; this defense prevents them from taking action which in turn protects them from attack. Their fundamental issue is dealing with fear and paranoia. There are phobic **Sixes** who avoid any- and everything that frightens them, but there are counter-phobic **Sixes** who deliberately embrace anything of which they are afraid. Rather than feeling the fear, they will tend to project it onto their environment. Their center of intelligence is the head and their most comfortable style of being is thinking.

Main Filter or Focus of Attention: Other people's hidden intentions, and potential danger.

Childhood Theme/Concern: Sixes couldn't trust authorities since adults were not reliable. They experienced punishment and humiliation. Parents were unpredictable and erratic. There were family secrets. They needed to predict the adults' behavior in order to protect themselves. **Sixes** experienced a sense of powerlessness to act in their own defense, and there was no strong figure to offer protection. Authority figures were cold and could be violent.

Personality Traits: Sixes are intuitive, loyal, hardworking, and possess strength and power. They are serious, self-sacrificing, and have powerful imaginations. Although they don't have many friends, they are very faithful to those they do have and tend to have longterm relationships. They are mindful of tradition and do not judge by appearances; they can see deep within a person. They tend to identify with the underdog. They produce best under pressure. Phobic **Sixes** will avoid perceived danger while the counterphobic **Sixes** will embrace it, throwing themselves into anything they are aware of fearing—meeting the tiger on the path. Centered in the head, **Sixes** have difficulty making decisions because of self-doubt. Afraid of direct anger and suspicious of others motives, they seek safety in structure. There is great difficulty in doing—in completing goals—because of that strong self-doubt and questioning of self. **Sixes** will procrastinate and move away from action, avoiding the possibility of imagined future attack. **Sixes** have a great deal of anxiety, fear of intimacy, and difficulty trusting because exposure makes them vulnerable to attack. To maintain self-esteem, they become defensive and overcompensate by acting forcefully. Thinking replaces doing; hence, the ambivalence and procrastination. They tend toward non-stop talking and noticing what's wrong; they can become paranoid and extremely insecure and anxious. Negative memories are more available than positive memories. They are dichotomous, either/or thinkers, and this supports a certain amount of rigidity.

Typical Beliefs: Getting close is dangerous. Visibility/ exposure is dangerous. Nothing is what it seems. Vulnerability leads to hurt. One must always be prepared. Life is dangerous.

Typical Compelling Question: "What am I missing?" "What will this cost me?" "Am I in danger?" "Can I trust?" "What is really going on?" "What is going to get me next?"

Boundary Issues: There are walls between **Sixes** internal and external worlds, and around feelings and intimacy.

Attention Shifts for Personal Evolution: Sixes must

acknowledge the tendency to project their fears onto the environment, realize that thinking replaces feelings, and stop blaming others and self. They need to appreciate self and others, recognize aggression as a signal of fear, and stay connected even when afraid. As they create more balance and permeability between thinking, feeling and doing they will transform walls into boundaries. **Sixes** should become more comfortable with visibility; through maintaining a sense of personal safety even when exposed, they can support their self-esteem.

Specifics: **Sixes** need to stay with projects and complete them; they need to challenge and develop choice regarding their internal self-doubting voice. The therapist should assist them to learn to match and move towards, to challenge their mind reading. **Sixes** need to witness and connect with emotions—especially fears. Identify and pay attention to positive memories and accomplishments. Reality-check intuitions. **Sixes** will benefit from becoming more aware of their tendency to dissociate and should develop the choice to associate when appropriate. They should sort by people and activity more, become more active, less passive.

VIGNETTES

During an advanced seminar on the Enneagram and NLP, we had been discussing the personality traits of a **Six**. A participant asked about the tendency toward paranoia, and I turned to one of my colleagues who is very aware and knowledgeable of the Enneagram, and asked her to answer the question. As she is a **Six**, I would be getting my answer from the horse's mouth, so to speak! Her immediate reaction was to put her notebook in front of her face. She and I and the entire group began to laugh—recognizing that instinctive gesture as indicating the **Six's** discomfort with visibility and exposure. Of course, I inadvertently put her on the spot by asking her to describe her personal experience as a **Six** regarding paranoia. It was a wonderful example of a **Six**, who then went on to answer the question brilliantly and in great depth.

* * * * *

At another Enneagram Seminar there was a very high percentage of **Sixes** in the group—and every single one of them sat close to the door!

CASE HISTORIES

Dick L. is a counterphobic **Six** who relies on his mind and sharp perceptions—a thinker. He believes that life is dangerous. In our first session he related a dream in which he went to his father for a gun, "the big gun," and faced up to the menacing Tiger. As Dick L. stated, "Lots of things are scary but **I often choose not to avoid them, to prove myself brave.**"

Like many **Sixes**, Dick L. hails the underdog and takes a long time to trust. After a very difficult divorce, he left his abusive roots in the South and befriended Alice. After years of being friends and now roommates, they have just celebrated a decade of loyalty. For a **Six** to accomplish this level of trust is difficult. Using Alice as a role model for change, Dick L. has gained more confidence in his own ability to change.

Dick L. is feisty and determined and he has achieved many of his outcomes in our therapy work together. In addition to his going-for-the-gun dream, he also discussed the movie *Cape Fear* in our first session. His outcome was to experience fear and anger appropriately. He describes his family as the Addams Family, with a large dose of violence and stupidity. His natural mother died while giving birth to him and he was adopted by a couple that he refers to as "dangerous" parents. His adopted father is the youngest of twelve, a closet gay alcoholic who beat him throughout his childhood. His adopted mother is from a blue-collar cotton-mill family who, when not participating in beating him, ignored him. My client describes his mother as a "vicious little pet." Dick L. was a rebellious child with a "fuck authority" attitude. When his parents almost divorced, he was asked which parent he wanted to live with. As he reports, "I chose my father; I would rather be beaten than ignored." When Dick L. asked to go to college, his parents, who thought higher education unnecessary, were eager to send him to trade school. "My parents made success difficult."

Dick L. has continued to seek education and information. He is a writer and has just received an assignment from a major national magazine and has recently signed a contract with an international publisher. Horror is his writing genre of choice. As he eloquently states, "No other literary style offers so many creative options—so many colors, so subtle and sharp. Horror is the handbook of the unconscious. The magician casts a magic circle, and enters space where time is a luminous liquid . . . in horror, you are already there, simply by using the rich, evocative symbols of the genre. Trees dance, houses eat little boys . . . we get to dream with our eyes open. Some of the dreams are erotic . . . all have potential for life. It's scary. No other genre requires so much courage . . . we find out that not only is the emperor naked, he's doing five to ten for exposing himself on the playground. Then we find out: maybe the emperor is us."

Dick L. has learned to make his world safe and creative. His anger and fear are appropriately placed in his life and his literary works. After his abusive childhood, in which he was raped, and after a marriage ending in a divorce, he is claiming his path of evolution.

* * * * *

Bobbie Z. is a 21-year-old woman who sought therapy following the breakup of the relationship with her first lover. Her overall style in life was marked by "hypervigilant self-protection"; this attitude resulted in no one at work knowing anything about her private life and vice versa. The ex-lover was also a co-worker, which in her experience was a significant boundary violation and generated tremendous anxiety.

At this same time Bobbie Z. started having increasing conflict with her best friend, who was also her roommate and who was preparing to get married. She slowly became aware that her hurt about her friend's "disloyalty" was more about her feelings of being replaced. Because direct conflict was so difficult for her, she avoided expressing her feelings openly to her friend, and this created distorted mindreading on both sides.

She had difficulty in recognizing her emotions and expressing them; she was very frightened of crying, of being angry, of helplessness and of most other intense emotions. At the beginning of therapy, she cried throughout the entire session, but reported feeling nothing and having no idea why she was crying. Whenever any intense issue came up, and/or she cried, she repeated being unable to think about or talk about anything, and when she did think or talk, she said she couldn't feel anything. Bobbie Z. was caught in a typical either/or: I can think **or** feel—but never both at the same time. This is an example of severe walls between head and body.

Therapy began to move her toward experiencing her feelings, at the moment they occurred, and using them as allies to help her feel strong, to express herself more directly to others, thus creating boundaries between thinking and feeling. This new awareness allowed her to think **and** feel.

THERAPEUTIC APPROACH FOR SIXES

Sixes' fundamental strategy for survival and safety is to be prepared for any possible type of future attack. "If I'm prepared I'll be safe." This strategy results in an innate desire to be invisible, not risk exposure and to procrastinate about completing projects, thus avoiding the challenge and risk of new ones. They embody self-doubt and a preoccupation with fear—either embracing danger (counterphobic **Sixes**) or avoiding risk (phobic **Sixes**). Their core issue is **fear**. **Sixes'** basic defensive position is away from exposure and their center of intelligence is the **head**—using thinking to protect themselves. The traditional, psychological diagnosis is paranoia. Described in NLP terms, **Sixes** mindread, tend to be dissociated, pay attention to their own and others' internal processes, lack boundaries between their internal and external worlds and their general direction is away from. Often **Sixes** suffered abusive childhoods—sexual, physical or at the very least verbal abuse. Therapeutically, they need guidance to learn to tolerate fear and develop forgiveness, to trust themselves and others, and to develop doable goals and complete projects. **Sixes** need to become more comfortable with visibility, deal with their self-doubt, establish healthy boundaries, value others' reality, check out the validity of their projections, and stop blaming self and others.

NLP PATTERNS
(see Appendix 1 for definitions)

Mismatch
Mind Read
Sort by Information
Move Away From
Passive

Polarize to External Frame of
   Reference
Dissociate
Attend to Own and Others
   Internal Processes
Primary Representational
System: Auditory
Criterion: Courage

SPECIFIC NLP THERPEUTIC INTERVENTIONS

As therapists we have found that the progress and evolution of our clients depends upon three categories of development: **Boundaries, Beliefs** and **Criteria,** and **Internal/External Worlds**. Since the Enneagram system is a dynamic one, the limitations and challenges of each personality type fall into issues relating to boundaries; to negative beliefs and conflicting and/or rigid criteria; and to a preoccupation with either the inner or the outer world which results in an imbalance and/or impaired relationship between the two. Therefore we have organized our interventions within these categories.

BOUNDARIES
• Use the **Boundaries Model and Process** to help **Sixes** establish appropriate boundaries regarding their paranoia.
• For severe cases of paranoia, use the **Trauma Phobia Process**. This technique can be done for early events of trauma or more recent ones, and alleviates acute stress and fear.
• Using the **Perceptual Positions Process** help **Sixes** develop alternative views of people and the world outside that appear so threatening and dangerous.

• Teach **Sixes** the **Index Computations**; have them become aware of how often they focus on their own internal processes and dissociate. Have them stay associated to their bodies and emotions.

BELIEFS & CRITERIA
• Identify limiting beliefs, especially those around "life is dangerous," and shift these to more supportive beliefs. Use the **Reimprinting Process**.

INTERNAL/EXTERNAL WORLDS
• Use the **Smart Outcomes Model** to create goals, to motivate **Sixes**, and to encourage them to stay with and complete projects—avoiding procrastination and creating the ability to move toward.
• Use **Change History Process** so **Sixes** learn to appreciate their "okay-ness" in painful childhood experiences.
• Use **Reframing (6-Step)** to identify the good intention behind self-doubt. **Sixes** will then begin to shape a more positive relationship with the self.
• Use the **Spacial Reframe** to resolve inner conflicts between parts. This technique serves to strengthen positive self-esteem.
• The **Fair Witness Position** can be effective in helping self-esteem and alleviating self-doubt.
• Develop awareness and choice in **Sixes** so they do not to have to take the defensive stance of mismatching out of fear. Teach them how to match. Challenge and use their ability to be courageous to motivate them to learn to match. If they can manage that, have them match authority figures with whom they are fearful and tend to avoid.
• Teach them to recognize their tendency to mindread; consistent reality checks are essential for mental and emotional health.
• Use the **Reclaim Personal History Process** to recall and reinforce positive memories, accomplishments and resources. Future-pace these resources and place on the future **Time Line**.
• Use **Submodality** processes to enable them to have more choice about their emotion of fear.

SEVEN: THE RENAISSANCE-PLAYER

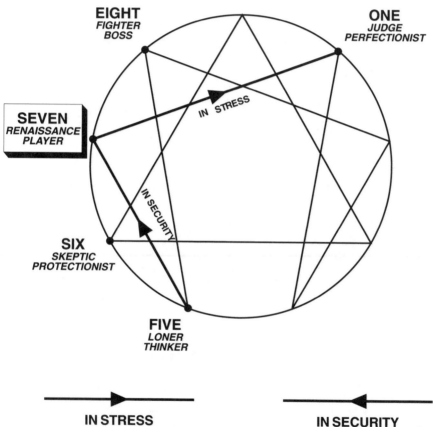

EIGHT
FIGHTER
BOSS

ONE
JUDGE
PERFECTIONIST

SEVEN
RENAISSANCE
PLAYER

IN STRESS

IN SECURITY

SIX
SKEPTIC
PROTECTIONIST

FIVE
LONER
THINKER

IN STRESS
Pointed end of arrow indicates the
direction of movement in stress.

IN SECURITY
Open end of arrow indicates the
direction of movement in security.

NOTE: The way that each individual defines and gives meaning
to the words Stress and Security is idiosyncratic. Stress
is not necessarily experienced as negative and security is
not necessarily experienced as positive.

Chapter 9

SEVEN: THE RENAISSANCE-PLAYER

Sevens are the Renaissance-Players. Their wing is either the Skeptic-Protectionist (Six) or the Fighter-Boss (Eight). In stress they move to the Judge-Perfectionist (One) and in security to the Loner-Thinker (Five). They are chiefly concerned with enjoyment, pleasure, and having choices; they avoid painful memories or emotions and any kind of commitment that remotely feels like a trap. Their primary defense is overindulgence, acting out and rationalization. Their fundamental issue is fear of being deprived, which they avoid by self- indulgence and pleasurable pursuits. Their center of intelligence is in the head and their most comfortable style of being is doing.

Main Filter or Focus of Attention: Many pleasant options and/or happy memories.

Childhood Theme/Concern: Sevens have had frightening childhoods which they dealt with by escaping into limitless possibilities of imagination and fantasy. They tend to retain only pleasant memories of childhood. There is a happy picture-book quality to their impressions and memories. Often the mother is narcissistic. Pain could not be expressed so they pretended everything was fine.

Personality Traits: Sevens are renaissance figures; adventurous and multitalented. They are optional, creative thinkers, who are extroverts, popular, self-sufficient and non-conformists. Talkative, gourmets, socially skilled, they like high levels of excitement, are stimulating and fun to be around, love to party and be the center of attention. **Sevens** are often known for their words, not for their deeds. They are good planners who move to future possibilities and pleasure; most of their excitement is at the beginning of a project, not in following through. They can be dilettantes—the "eternal child" or the "dance-away lover." They lack self-discipline and can get addicted to emotional and physical highs. Male **Sevens** often seek oral gratification and women are a high priority—sometimes they become womanizers. They have a lot of trouble with commitment, and must always experience themselves as having options, intimacy is avoided by holding on to options. Dreams and fantasy are much more attractive and rewarding than reality, than actually taking action. **Sevens** tend to be on the run—fast tempo, avoiding boredom at all costs. Seeking the new and the different, they tend to do many things simultaneously, exploring widely but not deeply. This pattern of avoidance supports their fear of not being as good as they want to be. They are narcissistic, rebellious, dreamers, and deny having any problems—especially emotional. Negative feelings cannot be tolerated. **Sevens** have an evenness of emotionality and an attitude of not taking life too seriously which masks deep emotions. They have many relationships and careers. The dynamic of a **Seven** is similar to 19th century French intellectuals chatting in cafes, delighted at providing inspiration rather than perspiration to society.

Typical Beliefs: Everything works out. Life is a feast. Choice is freedom. Commitment is a trap. I'm entitled. No options is death. More is better.

Typical Compelling Question: "What's here for me?" "What makes me feel good and how can I feel better?" "Am I as good as I think I am?"

Boundary Issues: Sevens lack boundaries between the present and future, between fantasy and reality. They have walls between thinking and feeling, and walls between different contexts of life; i.e., they compartmentalize their lives.

Attention Shifts for Personal Evolution: Sevens' evolution depends upon developing self-discipline and the ability to tolerate and learn from uncomfortable and painful emotions. It is important for them to stay with something through time and develop more awareness of the consequences of their behavior. They need to develop boundaries, especially between the present and the future, and around problems and the resulting painful or unpleasant feelings. Their challenge is to balance commitment and options, accepting that the two can exist simultaneously. **Sevens** need to develop depth: depth of emotions, commitment, inner awareness, and spirit.

Specifics: **Sevens** need to become more pro-active, especially regarding their own development and completion of projects. They should learn to be other-oriented and develop their kinesthetic/emotional systems. They need to acquire the choice to be through time; to recognize that beginning a new project may be their way to avoid something is essential. **Sevens** should increase sensitivity and awareness of the impact that their behavior has on others' internal state. They should challenge overindulgence; slow down; and deal with fears—challenge and adjust their complex equivalence for the commitment and pleasure criteria.

VIGNETTES

An extremely successful businessman in his late 50s who has pursued many courses in self-improvement and self-awareness was taking a Practitioner Training in NLP. Alert and fully concentrated, he enjoyed the course and was very enthusiastic about what he was learning. However, as the training progressed, issues and emotions were presented—and he began to fall asleep during the demonstrations. Disturbed by this, he kept saying that he was not bored and that the information and learnings were important to him. But he continued to fall asleep. The teacher explored this issue with him by communicating with the part of him responsible for him falling asleep. Together they discovered that this part was trying to protect him from any painful emotions and/or memories that might be accessed when watching a demonstration. The part agreed to allow him to stay awake if he promised to work **only** on superficial issues in class, and bring anything more important into his therapy sessions. He made this commitment to that part of him, and as a result was able to stay awake throughout the remainder of the training. He, of course, was a **Seven**!

* * * * *

A professional speaker and lecturer was describing how much more work she was getting, to the extent that she was being forced by her busy schedule to plan and commit to engagements even a year in advance. She said, "I hate to commit myself so far in advance—it feels like a trap!" She laughed and then said, "That's my **Sevenness** speaking."

* * * * *

Helen was talking about why she was so sure she was a **Seven**. For many years, she said she had thought of her childhood as absolutely idyllic—a storybook experience. Then Helen began to talk to her sister, who looked at her as though she was from another planet when she described her memories of their childhood. Her sister had very different memories and began to remind Helen about various situations and experiences. As her sister talked, Helen started to remember the painful and frightening aspects of her younger life. At that point Helen realized that she had totally distorted what had actually been a rather fearful childhood.

* * * * *

A **Seven** client who was beginning therapy said to her therapist, "I'd eventually like to experience all the therapists at this clinic." There were six.

* * * * *

Sam H. always starts his therapy session with a variation of "Things are great . . . I'm having fun . . . I did really fun things this week." Even when he was rejected by a woman he truly cared about, Sam H. began the session the same way. Every time the therapist attempts to get him to recognize and talk about his feelings, he argues that feelings are not useful.

CASE HISTORY

Mark S. is very busy—a doer—who regards life as a grand buffet. Bright and informed, he scurries from one activity to another. In a single day he has been known to go from tap class, to a tennis game with a friend, to a dance company rehearsal and to stripping cars. In the last few years, he has also trained horses, taken up golf, studied voice and jazz, trained professional rugby teams and become a certified masseur. Like most **Sevens** I have worked with, Mark S. is addicted to his own adrenaline. As another **Seven** client said, "If I was forced to do one thing, I would teach. I could teach many topics."

Mark S. views his life through a veil of options, holding fun as a major criterion. He admits, "I know how to be interesting and hold attention." Mark S. enjoys pleasing others, is socially adept and projects a sense of self-assurance. However, his inner voice is often comparing him to others and noting how he measures up.

In therapy, Mark S. talks often of open-ended plans and how commitment is a trap. For him, routine means boredom. In one session, I had Mark S. walk in a ten-step sided square for twenty minutes. He was not allowed to speed up or slow down. At first, he found this task to be an ordeal. However, he began to discover variety in this task and was delightfully surprised that routine does not have to be boring. Mark S.'s realization that always seeking variety is in itself a routine was significant in his therapy. It became important to Mark S. to focus on a few of his many talents and develop them more thoroughly. In the beginning of our therapy work together, he was a member of a dance theater company. He reported how difficult the choreographer was and each week he vowed to quit. Mark S. learned to accept the hard times and not to slither out the back door of his commitment. He saw it through in times of both pain and pleasure. His commitment to remain in the company for ten years broke through the major barrier of "boredom" and Mark S. is now on the road toward involvement and intimacy.

Like Peter Pan who ended up with a handful of wishes and no realities, Mark S. struggled with his wall between the present and the future. Spur-of-the-moment desires were given more through time consideration. His tendencies toward self-oriented goals have expanded into larger overview goals. At this time, Mark S. is engaged to be married.

THERAPEUTIC APPROACH FOR SEVENS

Sevens' fundamental strategy for survival and safety is always to have pleasant options. "If I have a lot of choices, I'll be safe." This belief results in an avoidance of commitment, unpleasant memories, and painful emotions. There is a reliance on positive future possibilities, a lack of self-discipline, and completion of projects with a deep, often unconscious negative self-esteem and self-distraction. The core issue for **Sevens** is fear. Their basic defensive position is away from commitment and their center of intelligence is the head—using thinking and new ideas to maintain pleasure and choices. The traditional psychological diagnosis is narcissistic. In NLP terms, **Sevens** are dissociated, especially from any painful emotions and/or memories; they move **toward** pleasure, sort by **self**, are in **time** and **passive** regarding their own problems and evolution. Therapeutically, **Sevens** must commit themselves to the therapeutic process, honor and fulfill the therapeutic contract. This commitment is the beginning of self-discipline.

Sevens will tend to treat the therapeutic process the way they do their life; by moving from one subject to another when things get too disturbing, or from one therapist to another when one gets too close to deep painful issues. They need guidance to learn to commit without feeling trapped, to stay with something and develop it in depth, to slow down enough to recognize and connect with painful emotions and problems, to develop a true relationship with their inner world and parts, and to develop the ability to identify and empathize with others.

NLP PATTERNS
(see Appendix 1 for definitions)

Toward	Visual
Self-oriented	Criteria:
Sort by Activity and	Pleasure and Choice (Toward)
Information	Commitment (Away)
Passive ("I wish")	Dissociated
In Time	Mismatch selves
Chunk Large	Fast Tempo

SPECIFIC NLP THERAPEUTIC INTERVENTIONS

As therapists we have found that the progress and evolution of our clients depends upon three categories of development: **Boundaries, Beliefs** and **Criteria**, and **Internal/External Worlds**. Since the Enneagram system is a dynamic one, the limitations and challenges of each personality type fall into issues relating to boundaries; to negative beliefs and conflicting and/or rigid criteria; and to a preoccupation with either the inner or the outer world which results in an imbalance and/or impaired relationship between the two. Therefore we have organized our interventions within these categories.

BOUNDARIES
• Use the **Boundary Model and Process** to help **Sevens** connect to their body and emotions; and to make distinctions between the present and the future.
• Use **Perceptual Positions Process** to enhance self-esteem and help them become more other-oriented, less self-absorbed. It teaches them to value and empathize with the other.

BELIEFS & CRITERIA
• Identify the beliefs connected to options and commitment and use the **Reimprinting Process** to change them.
• Identify the **Complex Equivalence** of commitment and use **Counter Examples** to eliminate feelings of being trapped, transforming commitment into pleasure.
• Challenge overindulgence. Can use **Criteria Spin**.

INTERNAL/EXTERNAL WORLDS

• Locate the resource of self-discipline and **Anchor** it as a positive experience. Find a time when self-discipline was fun and pleasurable. Establish it as a resource to go toward rather than away from.

• Develop exercises and tasks for **Sevens** to slow down, listen, and not dissociate—not just "walk through it."

• Use the **Smart Outcome Model** to establish goals and become motivated to stay with them. Most worthwhile goals cannot be attained in any depth without staying and dealing with the unpleasant or even painful emotions associated with them.

• Use **Time Line** work to help **Sevens** become more through time. Keeping a journal is also useful for this endeavor.

• Develop the desire for **Sevens** to become pro-active in their own development and in following through with projects. Change their modal operators to "I want" and "I will" from "I hope" and "I wish."

• **Reframe** (6-Step, or Spacial if there is an inner conflict) objections to getting in touch with unpleasant or painful emotions and memories. Use these processes also with objections to staying with something over time. This technique will also help to develop a supportive relationship with all their parts—even the painful ones.

EIGHT: THE FIGHTER-BOSS

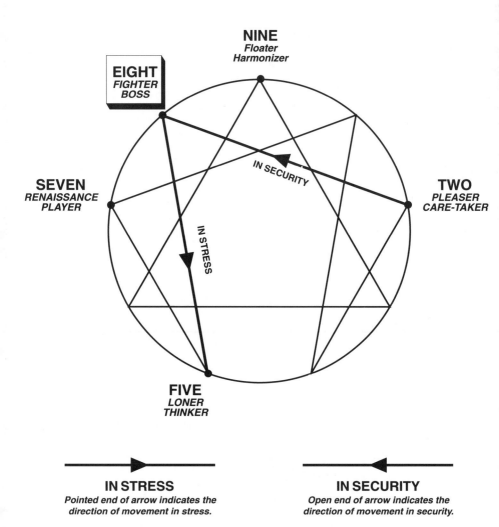

IN STRESS
*Pointed end of arrow indicates the
direction of movement in stress.*

IN SECURITY
*Open end of arrow indicates the
direction of movement in security.*

**NOTE: The way that each individual defines and gives meaning
to the words Stress and Security is idiosyncratic. Stress
is not necessarily experienced as negative and security is
not necessarily experienced as positive.**

Chapter 10

EIGHT: THE FIGHTER-BOSS

Eights are the Fighter-Bosses. Their wing is either the Renaissance-Player (Seven) or the Floater-Harmonizer (Nine). In stress they move to the Loner-Thinker (Five) and in security to the Pleaser-Caretaker (Two). They are chiefly concerned with power, strength and avoiding weakness. Their primary defense is denial and arrogance and their fundamental issue is anger, which they use to make contact and resort to instead of thinking. Their intellectual center is in the gut and their most comfortable style of being is doing.

Main Filter or Focus of Attention: Control.

Childhood Theme/Concern: Eights had combative or harsh childhoods, dominated by bigger, stronger people who wanted to control their lives. There was a sense of struggle against unfair odds. They learned that the only way to gain respect was by not showing weakness, by being strong. Sometimes **Eights** have experienced parental violation or a violent street culture—inner city and/or environmental. The reward for weakness was rejection; the reward for strength was success. The other common type of childhood was that parents were too liberal or soft and did not or could not provide limits, so the children needed to keep testing and pushing in order to find the limits.

Personality Traits: Eights are leaders; with high energy they are initiators and promoters of new ideas/things. They are strong supporters of others and are defenders of the weak. Fairness and power are important values for them. They like to take charge, are protective of friends and family, and are very loyal to those they trust. Uncompromising, they push the limits, love challenges and look for the truth. **Eights** have a good ability to see through games people play. They are more sensitive than they appear—tough on the outside (streetwise), soft-hearted on the inside. They are extremely irritable, with volatile expressions of anger; they make contact through sex and confrontation. They function well in difficult situations, like to be the center of attention, and are driven to be sought after. Excessive tendencies, especially with food, alcohol, sex and drugs, push them to extremes; they are attracted to edge-of-life experiences. Sometimes lust takes the form of wanting to control others totally. Blaming externals a lot, **Eights** deny their own weaknesses. They have a low tolerance for frustration, and in order to avoid boredom they will create trouble. They have a fast tempo, try to achieve intimacy through fighting, and are possessive. Anger equals power for **Eights**, and intensity is very important. Anger can flare up quickly—and can be over in a flash. Larger than life, **Eights** take up a lot of space—and need to control their personal space. They are intuitive thinkers and respond from the gut. They tend toward dichotomous thinking: either/or, going to one extreme or another. Whatever **Eights** do, they go full speed ahead. They can be shrewd and ruthless in maintaining power and control.

Typical Beliefs: The world is a tough place. Only the strong survive. You've got to fight to live. I'm the only one who can do it right. You can only depend on yourself. You're either for me or against me. "Eat or be eaten."

Typical Compelling Questions: "Who's in charge here?" "Are you for me or against me?" "What does he/she want from me?" "What do I have to do to get what I want?"

Boundary Issues: Eights have walls between internal and external worlds, and between self and others. There is a loss of boundaries in intimate relationships between self and significant others.

Attention Shifts for Personal Evolution: Eights evolve when they develop more balance and boundaries between their inner world and external behavior; when they learn to think instead of fight, to let go of control and acknowledge their vulnerabilities and weaknesses—to look inward rather than blame externals. The recognition of denial and the ability to go beneath it and deal in an in-depth way with their own issues are essential for any real growth and development.

Specifics: Eights need to identify their real wants and to develop their internal processes—the internal auditory and visual systems; this awareness will develop their choice to sort by information. Becoming comfortable with the choice to be receptive-passive will make **Eights** more balanced. They must become aware of denial as a signal to look deeper and inward. They need to acquire flexibility with boredom and tolerance for frustration; they need to challenge the either/or position and develop optional, non-polar thinking.

VIGNETTES

Nina is a middle-aged, successful professional who, before she learned about the Enneagram and recognized that she was an **Eight**, remembers saying often, "You've got to fight to live," and to her children, "It's you and me against the world." Nina's birth was difficult—her mother was in labor for over twenty-four hours, and Nina weighing two and a half pounds when born—not breathing and no heart beat! It took her until she was 35, she reported, to learn she didn't have to fight for everything—and she still has to remind herself that sometimes she has the choice to sit back and just let things happen . . . an **Eight**!

* * * * *

Joe talked about a friend, an **Eight**, whose ultimate test for friendship was, "Can you go 'back to back' with them during a fight in a bar?"

* * * * *

A woman who is now an NLP Master Practitioner said that a lot of things about her life started to make sense after she discovered the Enneagram and learned she was an **Eight**. Awareness of being an **Eight** was a turning point in her life. Now she realizes that it was crucial for her evolution that she learn how to think and to use her brain, rather than always react from the gut or confront. When she first began to study NLP, she realized that it was very special and important to her. NLP gave her the specific tools to learn to use her mind and to think! She can still fight and confront and she is still an instinctual thinker, but now she has more balance.

* * * * *

An **Eight** mother whose 18-year-old son is also an **Eight** told an amusing and enlightening story. Her son was making toast, forgot about it, and then got very frightened when flames started shooting out of the toaster and the kitchen filled up with smoke. His mother came into the house shortly after, and he began to yell at her for not buying a new and better toaster! After a few moments they both looked at each other and laughed about their recognized **Eightness**.

* * * * *

In an advanced workshop on the Enneagram, we were experimenting with choosing just one **Eight** pattern to shift in different problem situations. The shift we chose to try out was moving from active to passive. During the role play, I observed that every single **Eight** in the group had profound difficulty simply leaning back and becoming more passive. When they did lean back, this change shifted several other patterns and immediately put them in touch with feelings of vulnerability. This shift was scary and difficult, but in all cases proved effective in solving each different problem situation.

CASE HISTORIES

Harry P. is the husband of a **Two** client of mine who announced, as he entered my office, that "something had to be done." His **Two** wife came in quietly and sat for most of the first session, allowing her husband to dominate the therapy conversation. Harry P. is large in girth and in height, with a commanding voice and great shocks of blond hair. For most of the session he held center stage.

As Harry P. became more comfortable and trusting, he became less concerned about controlling the situation and dominating the sessions. One of the outcomes for therapy was to establish better communication between himself and his wife. She complains he is a "tease" and often goes too far. "His humor is poignant and when he gets on a roll, I feel like I'm being run over by a truck at eighty miles an hour. I take it as long as I can, then I burst into tears and he blows up." He counters, "Yeah, then we have to analyze it the rest of the day. I want it out and over with. You know, I'm the kind of guy that likes to fuck, fight or leave. I want to get on with it."

As the therapy progressed, Harry P. became more tolerant and less explosive. He and his wife have developed "signals" which allow her to let him know he has gone too far with his teasing. In return, he has a private "signal" for her when her tone becomes too demanding.

Twos and **Eights** can be good companions in the process of evolution. Whereas the **Two** stays away from overt anger, the **Eight** often uses anger in an explosive and unproductive manner. Each type can teach the other about dealing with anger in a positive manner. With Harry P., the teasing and anger cycles were counterproductive, blocking intimate communication. Establishing non-verbal "signals" was a first step. With further work, Harry P. and his wife developed greater understanding and acceptance of each other's style of communication.

* * * * *

Bill W. is a 50-year-old man whose wife had to threaten

divorce in order to get him into therapy. He had no interest in the process initially, claiming that he had no problems of his own, nor did he contribute anything negative to the family situation. He appeared to be very impressed with his own importance. This self-importance was hard for his wife and children to deal with and caused serious authority conflicts at work. He was a pilot who also held a middle-management position with his airline. He had no tolerance for being told what to do or how to do it. He enjoyed challenging and testing his peers and superiors at work, particularly if he thought they were incompetent, and he could be quite hostile and provocative at times. He would then deny his own role and responsibility in whatever backlash resulted from his provocation.

Bill W. saw himself as a "hippie" trying to live in the corporate world, and he attributed his constant conflict with others to this clash in values. At first he refused to realize that his provocative style was a fight for recognition and acknowledgment, as well as for preserving his identity and maintaining a sense of potency.

Unfortunately for Bill W.'s family, his needs extended to intimate relationships as well. He was extremely impatient, resentful of having to attend to the children instead of having them attend to him, and was totally rigid about insisting that things be done his way and for his benefit and convenience. At times he would make these demands openly but for the most part he was manipulative and expected his wife and kids to automatically support his inflated sense of self. He would become explosively angry when they didn't. Bill W. indulged in this pattern of demanding behavior which had started with his parents and had continued through his first and second marriages.

Extensive therapy revealed Bill W.'s underlying hypersensitivity and fear of being vulnerable, and his tendency to protect himself by having rigid walls between himself and other people. He slowly began to recognize and take responsibility for his anger, instead of always acting out. He also came to recognize his role in the marital discord and to accept that there were things about him that needed to be changed. He began to face his denial for what it was, to learn about his inner-self, and to develop boundaries. The growing courage that enabled him to be more vulnerable has contributed greatly to a gradual improvement in his relationships with his wife and children and with his colleagues at work.

THERAPEUTIC APPROACH FOR EIGHTS

Eights' fundamental strategy for survival and safety is to fight and control. "If I'm strong and fight, I'll be safe." This attitude results in reacting instead of thinking, using anger as a way to connect to others and to control. **Eights** have a tendency to be excessive, to go to extremes and to engage in dichotomous polar thinking; they depend on their instincts rather than develop their ability to think. Their core issue is anger. **Eights'** basic defensive position is against vulnerability and coming from the gut as their center of intelligence; they are instinctual thinkers. The traditional psychological diagnosis is sociopath and borderline.

Described in NLP terms, **Eights** are all or nothing (Universal Quantifiers); they value power and control and are very proactive. They sort well by people, have a strong internal frame of reference, emphasize externals and delete inner problems. Therapeutically, **Eights** must confront this tendency to deny inner problems and to blame something or someone in the external world. They need to develop and value their internal world, to learn to think rather than always react and fight, and to have the choice to be passive and to connect to their vulnerability. **Eights** must develop boundaries and optional rather than polar thinking. Generally, **Eights** only come into therapy because of a loved one or an undeniable problem and will probably want to leave therapy once the more obvious difficulty has been solved. However, they can benefit greatly by staying with the process and developing more awareness and appreciation of their inner worlds.

NLP PATTERNS
(see Appendix 1 for definitions)

Match Kinesthetically
Mismatch Information
Pro-Active
Internal Frame of Reference
Move Towards

Attend to Self & Other
  External Behavior
Mind Read
Sort by People & Activity
Criteria: Power, Control,
  Loyalty and Fairness

SPECIFIC NLP THERAPEUTIC INTERVENTIONS

As therapists we have found that the progress and evolution of our clients depends upon three categories of development: **Boundaries, Beliefs** and **Criteria**, and **Internal/External Worlds**. Since the Enneagram system is a dynamic one, the limitations and challenges of each personality type fall into issues relating to boundaries; to negative beliefs and conflicting and/or rigid criteria; and to a preoccupation with either the inner or the outer world which results in an imbalance and/or impaired relationship between the two. Therefore we have organized our interventions within these categories.

BOUNDARIES
• Through **Index Computations** make **Eights** aware of their attention to the external world and their deletion of their own internal world.
• The **Perceptual Positions Process** gives them a strategy to dissociate and be in 2nd position—this dissociation provides them with space to think about their response instead of reacting automatically, usually with anger.
• Use the **Boundaries Model and Process** to encourage a more choiceful position; rather than swinging from walls to no boundaries. They will gain more flexibility and choice.

BELIEFS & CRITERIA
• Use the **Reimprinting Process** to transform the beliefs about strength, fighting and vulnerability.

INTERNAL/EXTERNAL WORLDS

• Use the **Smart Outcome Model** in order to establish what an **Eight** wants exactly and specifically.

• Use the **Eights'** criteria of power and control to motivate them to learn to be more passive—as in receptive. Use body posture: lean back—passive, or leaning forward—active.

• When in the receptive mode, have them **Model** someone who they perceive has power.

• Utilize the **Fair Witness Position** and **Non-Polar Thinking Exercise** to develop optional, non-polar thinking.

• Use **Changing Expectations Process** to give them more choice about their reactions related to issues of control.

• **Reframe** (6-Step or Spacial if there is inner conflict) objections to becoming more passive, not fighting, or to looking inward and taking responsibility rather than denying or blaming something external.

• Develop **Eights'** internal auditory and visual representation systems so that they have more choice about thinking instead of fighting.

• Give tasks and exercises to increase skills in sorting for information, thus developing thinking rather than reacting.

• **Submodality** work will direct **Eights'** attention inward and help them learn about their minds and how to think.

• **Eights** must deal with their tendency to go to extremes and be excessive instead of controlling their emotions and thinking. Tempo change work can be helpful. Identify the triggers that provoke anger and fighting. **Anchor** a resource that supports thinking and choice to those triggers.

NINE: THE FLOATER-HARMONIZER

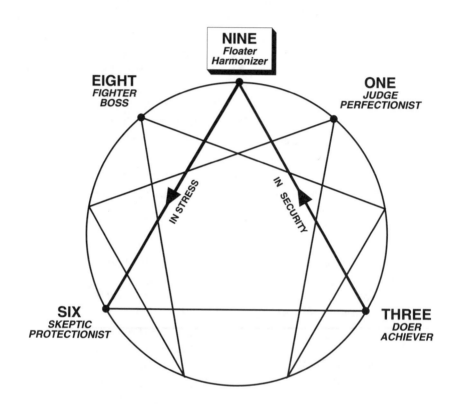

IN STRESS
*Pointed end of arrow indicates the
direction of movement in stress.*

IN SECURITY
*Open end of arrow indicates the
direction of movement in security.*

NOTE: The way that each individual defines and gives meaning
to the words Stress and Security is idiosyncratic. Stress
is not necessarily experienced as negative and security is
not necessarily experienced as positive.

Chapter 11

NINE: THE FLOATER-HARMONIZER

Nines are the Floater-Harmonizers. Their wing is either the Fighter-Boss (Eight) or the Judge-Perfectionist (One). In stress they move to the Skeptic-Protectionist (Six) and in security to the Doer-Achiever (Three). They are chiefly concerned with harmony and avoiding conflict. Their primary defense is slowing down, becoming unfocused and ambivalent. Their fundamental issues are anger turned inward and a denial of the essential self. Their center of intelligence is in the gut and their most comfortable style of being is feeling.

Main Filter or Focus of Attention: Other people's positions or point of view.

Main Childhood Theme/Concern: Nines often felt overlooked and neglected, sometimes overshadowed by siblings. Their families often prevented effective expression of their anger and desires. **Nines** had the sense of not being listened to and often felt caught between two opposing factions. They learned to space out to deal with uncomfortable emotions, especially anger. They had the impression that their parents' interests were more important than theirs. They felt disregarded and not valued.

Personality Traits: Nines value peace and harmony and have a calming influence on a situation. They are stable, cheerful, friendly, balanced, gentle, caring and good sleepers. They are extremely intuitive. They dream of the ideal mate, and union with a beloved is extremely important. Their connection with others is essential and they maintain this connection by identifying with the other, often even becoming the other. In the

Nine personality, the ability to see another's point of view reaches its zenith. This ability often results in extreme ambivalence and passivity. Socially and in a group, **Nines** can appear to be good listeners—but they often float in and out of conversations. They are good peacemakers and counselors are supportive of family and friends. They handle emergencies well. They appear to be in equilibrium and yet often are asleep and deaf to their own needs as individuals. They have trouble standing up for themselves—saying no. Self-deadening can be accomplished with too much food, TV, alcohol, gambling, and indiscriminate sex. **Nines** have difficulty making decisions and establishing priorities. They avoid conflict and sweep problems under the carpet. Completing things and staying with their goals is difficult for them because they distract themselves with inessentials. Taking each action deliberately and slowing down is their method of control. Their anger is expressed indirectly and directed inwardly, sometimes resulting in self-punishment or injury. Another form of anger turned against self is a **Nine's** tendency toward self-deprecation; they can be jealous and possessive. They tend to merge with others kinesthetically—merging with others leaves them feeling drained. Some **Nines** have trouble living with another because of the loss of autonomy. Time alone is important, enabling them to reconnect with themselves. They vacillate between compliance and defiance and can be very stubborn. Blaming others and external circumstances, they often do not take responsibility for themselves. They avoid planning for the future and meeting deadlines; they like the familiar and can fall into a life of habit and repetition.

Typical Beliefs: Others' needs are more important than their own. Everything has value.

Typical Compelling Question: "Am I making the right choice?" "Do I agree or disagree?" "What if ...?"

Boundary Issues: Nines lack boundaries between their internal and external worlds, and between self and other intimate relationships.

Attention Shifts for Personal Evolution: Evolution for **Nines** consists in establishing priorities and staying with them, developing a stronger internal frame of reference and standing up for themselves. It is important for them to concentrate on their outcomes; to learn to tolerate confrontation and conflict, rather than spacing or going numb. Creating boundaries between their internal and external world and between self and others will provide the separation they need to recognize what is important for them and what it is that they want from themselves. Challenging their tendency to fall asleep to their own essential selves will create the proper boundaries for healthy connections with others.

Specifics: **Nines** need to become more pro-active. In order to appreciate themselves more, they must learn to match self. **Nines** need to initiate and complete projects, to challenge self-distractions as a way to avoid doing. They need to develop choice to be self-oriented (ability to say no) and to recognize and acknowledge their own wants and needs. They need to learn a sense of the future by developing smart outcomes, by challenging complex equivalences of conflict. **Nines** need to develop the ability to recognize and express appropriate anger, and to realize that numbing themselves is a signal of anger. They should stop slowing down or spacing out as a way to control.

VIGNETTES

During my introduction to the Enneagram, I was struck with an immediate and strong recognition upon reading about **Nines'** strategy of slowing down to control. I remember my daughter's tendency even at age five or six to slow down when we would go shopping. The faster I would go, the slower she got. It would drive me crazy as I am an Eight! My daughter is now in her mid-twenties, and on a recent vacation we had a rather complicated change of planes to make at a large airport. Our time was tight, so I became very efficient and quick. The faster I moved, the slower she got! I would be halfway across a busy concourse and when I looked for her, she was trailing far behind. With the understanding gained from the Enneagram, I was able to observe myself and her and laugh! It was so predictable! However, I must admit that despite my laughter, I was annoyed at the moment the slowing down happened. Ah well, just one more way for me to evolve!

* * * * *

One of my dearest and closest friends is a **Nine**. Amelia A. is smart, loving, fun, creative and very sensitive. We connect deeply on every level that counts. In one area, I used to get very annoyed with her. Occasiȯnally I (an Eight) would get angry and upset with someone, but over serious betrayals or painful experiences—not minor irritations. Despite Amelia W.'s sensitivity and loyalty to me, when I confided in her she would merely listen, sympathize with my hurt feelings, and **never** take my side. Never would she criticize the other! Before learning the Enneagram, I thought she was just being high-minded. Now I understand that being a **Nine**, she is compelled to see all sides and consider every point of view, for there is value in everyone's position. I no longer get annoyed or feel slightly betrayed.

CASE HISTORIES

Brock F. is a businessman and like most **Nines** strives to stay present, awake to his immediate environment and his essential being, yet he reports that he often "floats off" during meetings at work and in conversations with others. Even in therapy he admits he has difficulty staying focused. **Nines'** defense and protection from the pain of being neglected as children and not having their needs met was the strategy of "spacing out," not remaining present, and going to sleep to their essential selves. Our therapy work has concentrated on helping Brock F. stay associated and focused on the situation, person, or topic at hand.

Brock F. is highly sensitive and people-oriented. Like Twos, **Nines** merge with others and lose their boundaries of where they end and another begins. Twos merge to remain connected and to gain approval. Unlike Twos, **Nines** lose self-definition in these situations. Not only does this tendency to lose self-definition occur cognitively, but also in actual physiology. Brock F. reported that one evening after work he was feeling excited about the upcoming weekend with his wife—up until his daughter arrived. His daughter had experienced a very grueling day and was grumpy and exhausted. Brock F. reported that upon being with his daughter, almost immediately he became tired and listless. In a body-felt sense, **Nines** match another with precision, and until they become more aware and evolved they experience little choice.

With stubborn assertion, **Nines** can be superb mismatchers—especially with information or opinions. This pattern of mismatching can be a method of claiming individuality, almost an antidote to losing self-definition. Often the so-called opinion has little to do with cognitive decision-making or real feelings. As I was testing this pattern in casual conversation with B.F., I said that I really liked my new wall hanging quilt: did he? He said, "No, I really hate the prevailing colors of rose and purple." Sometime much later in the year, I mentioned that I was considering moving the quilt out of the office, and that he would probably be pleased since he didn't like it very much. As if we had never discussed the quilt before, he strongly said, "Oh, don't move it, I really like it."

The most recent therapy has involved Brock F. developing a stronger internal frame of reference. He has become more and more conscious of his habit of saying, "I don't know," and now recognizes that this can mean he has spaced out, dissociated from the situation, or is avoiding taking a stand. Not taking a stand, except when spontaneously mismatching, was safer until the recent development of an internal frame of reference. Six months ago, Brock F. found it difficult to choose a meal from a restaurant menu. Now he reports that he can remain alert, consult his stomach and his taste buds, and make a clear decision without being duly influenced by those around him.

When not evolved and stuck in the pattern of mismatching, **Nines** can tediously complain and blame. In early sessions, Brock F. found himself stuck in this blame cycle—refusing to follow and not taking the lead. He complained about his boss, "He was a bad manager, didn't know the ins and outs of the business . . . he strutted around the office giving orders and trying to impress people." In time, the boss's position was usurped. My client was next in line—and his immediate reaction was to sit back. Unaware **Nines** who haven't worked on evolving prefer to stay in a bad situation and blame others rather than take action by leaving or changing. Confrontation and action are difficult.

Anger stimulates action in a **Nine**. Even though they are slow in tempo, fury is key in motivating them. Brock F. has utilized his anger as a message, broken the blame cycle, and is at present conferring with his co-workers to reorganize the business under new management. Taking action instead of remaining passive is important in B.F.'s continuing evolution. Translating anger into a positive message for action and daily exercise are vital. Quoting my client, "After exercising on my bike, I feel clearer, more aware and can take action with more confidence and purpose." The only path toward evolution for a **Nine** is the one that revives the essential self.

THERAPEUTIC APPROACH FOR NINES

Nines' fundamental strategy for survival and safety is self-forgetting—ignoring their essential self. "If I'm not really here, I'm safe." This results in not really knowing what they want or standing up for themselves; in ambivalence and in difficulty making decisions—the result of a lack of a strong internal frame of reference and obsessive avoidance of conflict. **Nines'** core issue is anger. Their basic defensive position is against conflict, and they come from their gut as the center of their intelligence. They think instinctually and depend on their intuition. The traditional psychological diagnosis is passive-aggressive and obsessive. Described in NLP terms, **Nines** have internal critical auditory messages, an external frame of reference that they polarize to, and a strong moving away from conflict. Therapeutically, they must develop an internal frame of reference, appreciate themselves and create an inner structure for self-esteem, recognize when they're angry and express it appropriately, establish goals and learn to initiate and complete projects. They need to become more pro-active, develop self-discipline regarding numbing themselves out or distracting themselves, and become comfortable in maintaining comfortable boundaries.

NLP PATTERNS
(see Appendix 1 for definitions)

Other-oriented	External Frame of Reference
Sort by People	Passive
Third Position (the Other)	Attend to Self and Other
Kinesthetic (Emotional)	Internal State
Match Kinesthetically	Present Oriented
Mismatch Information	Downtime
Self and Others	Criteria: Toward Union, Peace
	and Harmony/Away from
	Conflict

SPECIFIC NLP THERAPEUTIC INTERVENTIONS

As therapists we have found that the progress and evolution of our clients depends upon three categories of development: **Boundaries, Beliefs** and **Criteria,** and **Internal/External Worlds.** Since the Enneagram system is a dynamic one, the limitations and challenges of each personality type fall into issues relating to boundaries; to negative beliefs and conflicting and/or rigid criteria; and to a preoccupation with either the inner or the outer world which results in an imbalance and/or impaired relationship between the two. Therefore we have organized our interventions within these categories.

BOUNDARIES
• Use **Change History Process** on **Nines'** past experiences that reinforce negative self-image—making distinctions between themselves and the opinions and values of others.
• Use the **Boundary Model and Process** to allow **Nines** to maintain separation and connection between their internal and external world and between themselves and others in intimate relationships.

BELIEFS & CRITERIA
• Identify limiting beliefs about anger, conflict and standing up for themselves. Use the **Reimprinting Process** on these and the

belief that "others' needs are more important than mine." This will establish an inner structure for self-esteem.

• Challenge the **Complex Equivalence** of their criteria of conflict and confrontation. Use **Counter-Examples** to expand these definitions and **The Spin** to get them to realize that by avoiding conflict they are jeopardizing their chances of attaining union and harmony. Union and harmony are won by expressing one's needs, staying alert to oneself and the other; this presupposes there will at times be conflict and confrontation.

INTERNAL/EXTERNAL WORLDS

• Help **Nines** to recognize anger when it arises by becoming aware of visual, auditory, and kinesthetic primary triggers that precede the anger.

• The **Spacial Reframe Process** has a powerful impact when working with **Nines'** ambivalent parts. In order to express their needs and wants, **Nines** need to become less ambivalent and more pro-active, match themselves, and become self-oriented— actually recognizing their own needs and wants.

• **Reclaim Personal History** strengthens the positive resources for knowing and getting what they want and their positive self-esteem.

• Teach them to recognize numbing out on TV, indulging excessive eating, etc. are signals that they are forgetting their essential self. That is the time when they must be alert to their own needs, express them, and fulfill them.

• Use the **Smart Outcome Model** to help **Nines** recognize and develop their goals. Challenge their tendency to distract themselves with the inessentials, to procrastinate, and not to finish projects. Provide exercises for doing, making lists and completing them.

• **Reframe (6-Step)** passivity and give them greater choice to do.

• Use **Timeline** work to create more of a sense of the future, use the **Reframe (6-Step)**to deal with their objections to being more future-oriented.

• Challenge their slowing down to control; use counter-examples to demonstrate the limitations of slowing down and the positive possibilities of maintaining at least a medium tempo.

• Biking, rollerblading, swimming, etc. are all excellent exercises for **Nines**. Held-in anger and frozen energy are released. Through the release of energy, the mind is cleared; it becomes more alert, and the essential self **wakes up**. For the **Nine**, waking up is the first step on the path to evolution.

PART II

APPENDIX 1

GLOSSARY OF NLP TERMS

Brief definitions or descriptions of all NLP terms used in this book are provided below.

Active: The type of involvement with others—the world; I do to the world—proactive, initiating.

Anchoring: The association of an explicitly created stimulus and a pre-determined response. Usually the stimulus is external: a specific touch, a specific word or sound, a specific gesture, expression or posture that is seen by the client. However, the stimulus can be internal: a thought, word or image. The purpose is to enable the therapist to hold steady and constant a positive and desirable response in the client in order to create new choices. Anchoring can also be done with one's self. (See also Self-Anchoring.)

Associated: All parts and sensory systems are inside the experience; being totally involved—no observer part. The person is totally involved, with no observer part.

Auditory System: The perceptual filter (sensory system) used to represent experiences, memories, thoughts and the sensory system that is favored consciously, that receives the most attention. In this case, the auditory: words, sounds, listening, etc.

Away: Refers to the direction that motivates the person and that the person is most conscious of: away from pain, failure, problems, etc.

Belief: A generalization about oneself and the world that defines guidelines about how to achieve or avoid a highly valued criterion. Beliefs propel all behavior, consciously and unconsciously.

Boundaries: (Boundaries, No Boundaries and Walls) Boundaries are those distinctions between internal and external experience, between self and others, and between different contexts. They are both permeable (allowing for the bi-directional exchange of information and emotions) and also sufficiently impermeable to maintain separation. In human experience, there can be No Boundaries if there is a lack of substantial distinctions and separation is lost and merger occurs. Walls are distinctions that separate but are not permeable, allowing no real bi-directional exchange of information and/or emotions and behaviors. (See Appendix 5.)

Chunk: In the cognitive process, chunk characterizes how one organizes experience into different sizes: small, medium, large. Chunk refers to information, emotions and behaviors, known sometimes as generalizations (large chunk) and details (small chunk).

Complex Equivalence: The detailed sensory specific description of what a person has to experience in order to have the experience of a value/criterion.

Congruency: All parts of the person are sending the same message so that the words and the external behavioral manifestations match. The words and other channels of communication (gestures, posture, facial expression, voice tonality and tempo, etc.) are conveying the same message.

Conscious: Refers to the mind that is aware of what is going on in any moment of time. The conscious mind is limited by its ability to notice/pay attention to seven plus or minus two (7 + 2) pieces of experience at a time. Sometimes referred to as the waking mind.

Counter-Examples: An example that does not fit a previous statement, generalization, or belief.

Criterion: A value that is used as a standard upon which to base one's evaluation or interpretation of an experience.

Deletion: Ignoring or eliminating parts of an experience, or information, in order to pay attention to other parts.

Distortion: A misrepresentation of the sensory stimuli present in an experience.

Dissociated: Some part of the person is in an observer position to himself and the experience. Watching/listening to oneself; being somewhat removed, outside of, distanced from an experience.

Downtime: Directing **all** one's conscious attention (7 ± 2) inward (as in trance or when daydreaming).

Ecology: Humans are an interlocking system of systems both within themselves (physiological, mental, emotional and spiritual) and outside themselves (family/intimate, job/profession, social/friends, community, and global). These systems constitute an ecology. Personal ecology registers the impact any change or adjustment will have upon the entire fabric of life.

External Frame of Reference: Refers to the fact that the locus of whatever value or standard being used to evaluate an experience is external (someone else's).

External Behavior: Primary conscious awareness of doing and talking, external body movements, any sensory external experience of self or other(s). One of the Index Computations.

Externally Oriented: Similar to UPTIME; however, not only is the person's focus of attention on external experience, but that is of primary importance to him/her.

Fair Witness Position: An observer position that is not detached; it is involved, accepting, and non-judgmental. (See Appendix 4.)

First Position: A position in which the reference point is inside self within an experience. One is seeing through own eyes, hearing through own ears, feeling own sensations, being emotionally impacted directly and immediately by the experience. First Position is a fully associated position.

Frames of Reference: Internal/External: Frame of Reference (**FOR**) refers to the locus of a value or standard being used to evaluate an experience; can be either internal (one's own) or external (someone else's).

Future-Oriented: Primary focus of attention and point of reference in the future time frame.

Generalization: A rule that defines the relationship between/ among experiences or pieces of experience.

Index Computations: Three distinctions in self and/or others' experience: Internal State (emotions), External Behavior (doing), and Internal Process (thinking).

Incongruency: When a part or parts of the person disagree with or have another opinion from that being expressed verbally. The words and the external, behavioral manifestations (gestures, posture, facial expression, voice tonality and tempo) do not match; the multilevels of communication are **not** sending the **same** message.

In Time: Refers to one's experience of time; freezing time so that everything stays the same. A person experiences virtually no possibility of change, whether it be over an hour, a day, a year, or ten years. Time and self become fully involved in the moment. If this occurs over time, there is difficulty learning and evolving, and one's self is experienced as static.

Inner Observer Part: A part of a person; the person that observes the self without judgment, from a non-polar position; similar to Fair Witness Position.

Internal Behavior: Making inner images, talking to oneself, listing to inner sounds and music, constructing inner sensation, tastes or smells.

Match: The cognitive process that results in noticing what is **there** in any experience; what fits together, is similar to, the same as, or is like something.

Meta Comments: An internal voice that comments on what a person is doing and or who a person is; sometimes critical.

Meta Outcome: The outcome of an outcome; the results of an outcome. Questions to identify Meta Outcome; "What is the outcome of that outcome?" "What will that outcome do for you? get you?" "What will that outcome accomplish for you?"

Mind Read: One of the nine patterns of the Meta Model, a linguistic model of patterns of generalization, deletion, and distortion. It presupposes that I know what you are thinking and/or feeling without any direct evidence; or the assumption that someone else knows what I am thinking and/or feeling without direct evidence.

Mismatch: The cognitive process that results in noticing what is **not** present in any experience; what is missing; what doesn't fit; isn't similar; is a counter-example or opposite.

Modal Operators: Certain words that modify and impact the mood of the main verb. The Modal Operator is one of the patterns of the Meta Model, a linguistic model of patterns of generalization, deletion and distortion.

Modal Operators of Necessity: A sense of urgency expressed in the main verb cluster; e.g., *have to, must, should, ought.*

Modal Operators of Possibility: Create a sense of what is possible; e.g., *want, can, will, able to.*

No Boundaries: The lack of substantial enough distinctions between internal and external experience, between self and others, and between contexts so that separation is lost and merger occurs.

Other-Oriented: Primary focus of attention and interest in other.

Parts: Aspects of one's personality that correspond either to the roles one plays in life (mother, brother, lawyer, teacher, peacemaker, troublemaker, etc.) or the significant and recurring emotions one experiences (caring, jealous, ambitious, fearful, etc.).

Passive: The type of involvement one has with others and the world as indicated by a receptive or reactive position. There is an attitude that the world "does" to me. A passive type can be anywhere within the spectrum from receptive to victim.

Past-Oriented: Primary focus of attention and point of reference in the past time frame.

Patterns: Any predictable sequence of behavior. A sequence can be a stimulus and associated response that is repeated predictably. This pattern can be external **and/or** internal as in thinking (images, words, sounds, sensation) and feeling.

Perceptual Positions: There are three perceptual positions: 1st, which is **Self**, the point of view of self; 2nd, which is **Observer**, the point of view of an observer; 3rd, which is **Other**, the point of view of the other. "Aligned" refers to possibility of all sensory systems aligned in one position: 1st, seeing, hearing and feeling from inside self; 2nd, seeing, hearing and feeling from inside observer; 3rd, seeing, hearing and feeling from inside other.

Perceptual Sorts: These are the perceptual filters the mind uses to organize which sensory aspects or parts of an experience it pays attention to consciously. They correspond to the five senses and the representational systems: Visual (seeing), Auditory (hearing), Kinesthetic (feeling), Olfactory (smelling), Gustatory (tasting).

Primary Sorts: These are the cognitive filters the mind uses to organize the type of experience it pays conscious attention to. They are Information, People, Place, Activity, Thing.

Polar Thinking: Dichotomous, "either/or" type of thinking: a system of thinking in which things are right or wrong, good or bad, with no grays, no options.

Polarize: Taking the opposite point of view to that being presented—polar thinking and reactions.

Positive Intention Function: There is a distinction between **behavior** and **intention**, and there is always some positive intention or function behind any internal or external behavior. This positive intention or function is related to the self only.

Present-Oriented: Primary focus of attention and point of reference in the present time frame.

Presupposition: That which is assumed to be true but not explicitly stated.

Representational System: The sensory system that a person uses to represent an experience, think about it, to remember it. There are five Representational Systems and they correspond to our five senses: Visual, Auditory, Kinesthetic, Olfactory, and Gustatory.

Second Position: This is the observer position in the Perceptual Positions in which the reference point is outside the experience. The person is watching him/herself, listening to him/herself, and having emotions **about** the experience. The emotions are somewhat removed from and detached from the actual experience. This is a dissociated position.

Self-Anchoring: The creation of an association between a stimulus and a desired response, when the person, him/herself, deliberately creates both the stimulus and the desired response. (See Appendix 4 for details.)

Self-Oriented: Primary focus of attention and interest in self.

Smart Outcome: An Outcome that is sensory-specific, ecological, contextualized, stated in the positive, and within the individual's control (a goal that is achievable).

Sort by: To select for, pay attention to, focus on, choose.

Sort by Activity: To pay attention primarily to the activities/doing connected to an experience.

Sort by Information: To pay attention primarily to the information/data connected to an experience.

Sort by People: To pay attention primarily to the people connected to an experience.

Standard: The value, criterion or reference used to evaluate an experience.

Submodalities: Aspects or qualities of each Representational System, also known as a submodality. For example: Visual (focus, size, light, distance, color, etc.); Auditory (tempo, volume, pitch, direction, etc.); Kinesthetic Primary (pressure, movement, temperature, etc.).

Subordinate Present for Future: Making the future more important than the present—denying or deleting what's happening in the present for the sake of something in the future.

Tempo: This refers not only to the tempo of speech but to the overall tempo (both the inner and outer tempo) at which a person lives his/her life: breathing, thought processes, inner voice, external movements, speech, etc.

Third Position: This is one of the Perceptual Positions and its reference point is within the other person: one is seeing through the other's eyes, hearing through the other's ears, allowing self to take on the other's sensations, posture, and emotion.

Through Time: Refers to a person's relationship with time that results in the experience of evolving change; awareness of movement through time, of the ever-changing effect time has on almost everything and everybody. One's self is experienced as an evolving process, and it is easier to learn and grow; however, it can also limit one's ability to become fully immersed in a moment of experience.

Time Line: Time and space are interconnected: For example, "Put that behind you" (Past); "Look ahead" (Future). Everyone has a conscious or unconscious spacial organization of their sense of personal time. This corresponds to a path, road, line that we travel over time. To simplify this, think of the past extending in a line either behind you or to the left and the future either in front of you or to the right, and the present either inside you or just a few inches in front of you. Make sure that this line is continuous from birth through the present and into the future far enough to be ecological.

Toward: Refers to the direction that motivates a person and of which the person is most conscious: toward pleasure, achievement, goals, success, etc.

Unconscious: Refers to the mind that stores all our experiences, knowledge, memories, etc., without our immediate awareness. In other words, everything we know and have experienced that we are not immediately aware of. Many parts of us remain unconscious (out of conscious awareness) much of the time but have specific and important functions with our overall inner system.

Universal Quantifiers: Words that indicate a polar position— categorical and limiting; an all or nothing; either/or approach (e.g.: *all, no one, everything, never, always*). This is one of the patterns of the Meta Model, a linguistic model of patterns of generalizations, deletions and distortion.

Uptime: Directing all one's conscious attention (7 + 2) externally. This is an ego-less state because the ego must be put aside in order to achieve it—there is no awareness of self, no self-observation.

Value: The standard used as a reference in order to evaluate an experience; same as a criterion.

Visual System: The perceptual filter (sensory system) used to represent experiences, memories, thoughts, and the sensory system that is favored consciously, that is paid most attention to. In this case, the visual—images, pictures, seeing, looking, etc.

Walls: Distinctions in the Boundaries Model that separate internal and external experience, self and others, and contexts, and are not permeable—allowing no real bi-directional exchange of information and/or emotions.

APPENDIX 2

ENNEAGRAM TYPE IDENTIFYING INTERVIEW

The purpose of this process is to identify the essential or core personality type and its wing. This interview is an interactive process; i.e., it is not a linear question/answer process, but a cybernetic process in which the therapist builds on the responses. Keep in mind the points to which each core type moves in stress and in security. The questions provided below are sample questions: you do not have to use all of them. Listen to the answers and begin to relate them to the different Enneagram core personality types by keeping in mind the way each type handles these different issues. Until you learn the aspect patterns, qualities, and themes of each type, keep referring to the nine type descriptions in this book.

When unable to decide between two or more types, explore how the person handles stress and security—and check this against the types in question. At first it may be useful to identify types by a process of elimination: identify the types the person is not. This narrows the possibilities down and facilitates the process. When using this process, be sure to assume a nonjudgmental posture (the Fair Witness Position).

Interview Questions

1. Describe your major childhood theme or concern.
2. Describe your relationship to commitment, both in general and in long-term relationships.
3. How would you know you were committed?
4. Describe your relationship to intimacy, to closeness.
5. How do you handle authority and authority figures?
6. How are your social skills? With groups/one on one?
7. What are your issues around control—how do you handle control?
8. What is your most comfortable or familiar style of being: Thinking/Feeling/Doing?
9. Describe your relationship with success.
10. Describe your responses to confrontation. To anger—both your own and others'? To fear?
11. How do you handle pressure? Stress?
12. Are you good at initiating projects, at finishing/completing projects?
13. Are you a head, heart, or gut person?
14. What are your strongest resources/assets/gifts?
15. Do you spend a lot of time in the past, present or future?
16. What is your self-image?
17. What do you avoid at all costs?
18. What is most important to you in life?
19. How do you evaluate and appreciate yourself?
20. What kind of conflicts do you habitually get into?
21. What are your habitual fears? Desires?
22. Explain what **trust** means to you. How do you establish trust with others? How do others establish trust with you?
23. Does doubt play an important role in your life? How do you experience doubt?

APPENDIX 3

ENNEAGRAM QUIZ
Derived from the work of Don Riso

In response to the following statements, remember that within each Enneagram core personality type there are different levels of evolvement, from less evolved to highly evolved. The **first nine** questions reflect **highly evolved** to **evolved traits**; the **second nine** reflect **evolved** to **less evolved traits**. Your level of evolvement can change within different contexts; e.g., personal, family, professional, social, etc.

Answer as spontaneously as possible without trying to figure out the right answer. To determine your type you will "mostly agree" or "strongly agree" with 12 to 14 of the 18 questions listed. **Most** of the statements of your type will describe you either in the **past**, as you are **now**, or as you could be in the **future**. Some of the statements may indicate only tendencies: either of your future potential or past limitations. Even if you no longer have those limitations, if you recognize them from your past, the appropriate response is to "agree." When you have relatively high scores in other core personality types, this may reflect your **Wing** or your **Direction of Stress** or **Security**.

This quiz is **not** a definitive process; rather it is simply another clue or guideline in helping you to determine your own or another's type. When doing the quiz, assume as much as possible a non-judgmental attitude toward yourself or the other (if giving someone else this quiz). The most effective position to take is that of Fair Witness.

ONES

1. I have high moral standards.
2. I have extremely good judgment.

3. I have a strong conscience that compels me to do what I think is right no matter the consequences.
4. I try to be as objective and fair as possible.
5. It is important to maintain my integrity at all costs.
6. I am generally stable and dependable.
7. I'm very well organized.
8. I like definite rules.
9. I do not like to get angry.
10. I strive for perfection in myself and others.
11. I am rarely satisfied with myself.
12. It's difficult for me to relax—some people think I'm a workaholic.
13. I am critical of myself and others.
14. I sometimes have trouble expressing my emotions— sometimes even recognizing or connecting to my emotions.
15. Things are either right or wrong.
16. I believe I have an obligation to let people know when they are wrong—and sometimes make sure they get what they deserve.
17. I can be obsessive.
18. I'm usually right about things—I'm never wrong about something important.

TWOS

1. I am empathetic and helpful.
2. My friends and friendships are essential in my life.
3. I understand people and am supportive of others, without concern about being rewarded.
4. Others well being is of central importance to me.
5. I'm happy when good things happen to others.
6. I'm able to draw out the best in people.
7. Love is the most important value in life.
8. I can be very intuitive.
9. Being needed is very important to me.
10. I give a lot to others so that I'll be loved.
11. I can be good at flattery and manipulating others—I sometimes try to control others by being of help to them.

12. I sometimes feel incompetent and lack confidence in my own abilities.
13. Half the time I don't really know what I want or know which of my many selves I really am. I think that by helping others get what they want, I'll get what I want and know who I really am.
14. Often I agree to help others—then I resent it and express it indirectly.
15. It's hard to let go of those who are important to me.
16. People take me for granted. They don't care about my needs.
17. I lose myself in others.
18. I get sick a lot.

THREES

1. I feel worthwhile and valuable.
2. I am my own best promoter. I can promote myself and my ideas.
3. I'm goal-oriented and can work well with others toward a definite goal.
4. I'm good at getting things done—at accomplishing things.
5. I'm positive and enthusiastic about life.
6. I'm good at planning the future.
7. I am persuasive and usually get my own way.
8. I like to run my own show—my work is very important to me.
9. I am impatient with incompetency and can be blunt and lack tact.
10. My appearance and how I impress others is very important to me.
11. I can be very domineering.
12. Success is essential—that's what gets you approval.
13. I'm superior to most people.
14. I don't like to get too close to people but need to be associated with many.
15. I need to be the center of attention.
16. I can use others to get what I want.
17. I'm obsessive about my work—some call me a workaholic.
18. My identity is my job/career.

FOURS

1. I have a lot of flair and style—a sense of the dramatic.
2. I am an artist at heart and like to surround myself with beauty.
3. My intuitive sense is well-developed.
4. I'm sensitive and imaginative.
5. I create worlds of fantasies that are very real to me.
6. I spend a lot of time having conversations in my imagination.
7. I am creative and my creativity is fed by my deepest emotions.
8. I like to analyze emotions—my own and others'.
9. I'm better one-on-one than with groups.
10. I dislike being thought of as ordinary—it is important that I am "special/unique."
11. People don't understand me—I'm different.
12. Things are either wonderful or horrible.
13. I have feelings of melancholy or depression—I am emotionally vulnerable.
14. I have a sense of inner shame. My inner voice can be very cruel and critical.
15. I often focus on the unobtainable or lost loves or dreams.
16. I'm envious of others success and/or happiness—other people always seem happier or more successful than I am.
17. I'm very self-absorbed.
18. Life is painful and full of suffering and isn't fair.

FIVES

1. I'm very insightful and perceive what others miss.
2. I can predict in advance the ways things will turn out.
3. I have many innovative ideas and thoughts.
4. The life of the mind excites me.
5. I have an excellent ability to concentrate—to become absorbed in my interests.
6. I want to know why and how things happen—I want to make sense out of the world.
7. I love the pursuit of knowledge—research and scholarship appeal to me.
8. I am good at rational thinking—logic is very important—I am an analytical person.

9. It's hard for me to become involved with others or make commitments; however, once I do, I am very faithful to a commitment.
10. I am a very private person—I'm usually not at ease in social situations.
11. I prefer being alone and relying on myself rather than others—it is safer and easier.
12. I need to know all the facts before I start something.
13. I like to observe—to remain the observer. I dislike being observed.
14. People sometimes describe me as an "egghead" or weird or eccentric.
15. I have trouble getting in touch with my emotions—and more trouble expressing them.
16. I distrust most people—especially those who have any power over me.
17. Most people are too stupid to understand me.
18. I prefer my fantasies to others' reality, even though these may be strange and frightening.

SIXES

1. I'm good at seeing beyond what's apparent, beyond what's obvious—I'm intuitive.
2. I care deeply about those to whom I am committed—I am a good and faithful friend.
3. I can inspire growth and development in my friends.
4. I'm reliable and a hard worker.
5. At my best, I'm creative intelligent and capable.
6. I can work with authority figures that I respect.
7. Other people find me lovable and sometimes want to protect me.
8. I have an off-beat sense of humor.
9. It's important for me to feel secure in my work and relationships; this sometimes makes me skeptical.
10. I am able to reason logically and like logical proof of things—I'm better with logic than I am with feelings.
11. I have trouble transforming my thoughts into actions and often procrastinate.

12. Sometimes I get very anxious—more than people realize.
13. I'm afraid of blame and often find excuses to avoid dealing with it.
14. Sometimes I've felt like I'm no good and don't deserve anything good out of life.
15. I often look for hidden dangers and can imagine and exaggerate problems.
16. I sometimes give people mixed messages—saying yes when I mean no, going along with something when I really don't want to.
17. I don't like people to dispute my reality.
18. I can be very suspicious of others and feel they don't like me and are out to get me.

SEVENS

1. Life is great—a feast just waiting to be enjoyed.
2. I'm a happy, spontaneous, full of life person.
3. I know a lot about many things—I'm multitalented—I'm really good at a lot of different things.
4. I'm practical and productive.
5. I like to be with people who are having fun. I'm fun to be around—I enjoy my friends.
6. I can create an adventure out of any experience.
7. I tend to be very uninhibited and outspoken.
8. I like to get attention.
9. I think of myself as a non-conformist and sometimes have trouble dealing with authority—I'm impatient and like action.
10. I've had a number of jobs/careers and/or many relationships.
11. I like to talk and tell stories—sometimes to the extent of forgetting to listen to others.
12. I avoid boredom at all costs—keeping busy is the way to go.
13. I go to extremes—feast or famine, mostly feast!
14. I believe you can never get enough of a good thing.
15. I can sometimes be an overconsumer of food, drugs, drink, sex, etc.
16. I'm often uncomfortable with emotions and avoid expressing disturbing feelings—or even feeling them.

17. Sometimes my life and I are out of control.
18. I'll do anything not to feel anxiety or depression.

EIGHTS

1. I'm strong, have stamina and a lot of energy.
2. I have a lot of self-confidence and assert myself.
3. I'm extremely persuasive—I command respect and am a natural leader.
4. I'm loyal to family and friends and will fight to protect them.
5. I'm deeply moved by the suffering of others.
6. I'm good at recognizing and promoting new possibilities.
7. I have a strong work ethic and can be demanding of myself and others.
8. I'm quick to anger and express it and respect those who stand up to me.
9. I like challenge and thrive on adventure—I often live on the "edge."
10. I'm often seen as tough—but I have a soft heart.
11. I'm decisive—I can make tough decisions.
12. It's them or me, and I'll fight to survive—to come out on top.
13. Money is important—if I have enough of it no one will have power over me.
14. I have great difficulty admitting to any weakness in myself.
15. I want to be in control of everything around me—not vulnerable.
16. It's good for people to fear you—the only thing people respect is power.
17. I can be ruthless and harbor revenge.
18. I'm the greatest and the most important person I know.

NINES

1. I like harmony in my relationships. I'm a peacemaker.
2. The mystical and contemplative dimensions of life are important to me.
3. I'm not judgmental and accept differences—I'm honest while trying to be diplomatic.
4. I'm balanced and stable.
5. I'm kind, gentle, and can have a soothing and relaxing influence on others.
6. My family—especially my spouse and children—are central to my life.
7. I'm very intuitive and connected to people.
8. I'm able to make others feel good—take care of them, and see their point of view.
9. I need to know what other people want—where they're coming from.
10. I want everything to be pleasant—I try to avoid conflict.
11. I sometimes have trouble knowing what I want; my interests can vary.
12. I can be stubborn.
13. I can space out easily—float through situations and experiences.
14. I have trouble asserting myself.
15. I sleep a lot and sometimes have low energy.
16. I have trouble motivating myself and staying with a goal.
17. I avoid facing unpleasant reality and thinking too much about the future.
18. I can overindulge in food, TV, etc. to avoid making a decision and doing something.

APPENDIX 4

NLP PROCESSES TO FACILITATE PERSONAL EVOLUTION AND THERAPEUTIC GROWTH AND CHANGE

Anchoring
Derived from the work of Richard Bandler & John Grinder

1. **Anchoring is an Associative Process**: a process that connects a specific stimulus with a particular response. It is sometimes called conditioning. We learn to connect/associate a stimulus, e.g., a tone of voice with a certain response, a feeling of comfort or anxiety. Because of people's ability to generalize—force of habit—the response kicks in even when the stimulus does not have the same meaning as the original; e.g., the tone of voice of a stranger does not necessarily have the same meaning as the tone of your mother or teacher.

2. **Aspects Important in Anchoring**
   a. Uniqueness of stimulus
   b. Intensity of response
   c. Purity of response
   d. Timing of anchor

3. **Anchoring Process**
   a. Use calibration skills to detect when a person is in an experience you want to anchor; using your behavior, facial expression, tonality, etc. congruently to elicit desired response.
   b. Make sure person is in the experience, not in meta-position (unless that is the experience you want to anchor). Watch eye-accessing, ask.

c. Anchor with touch, word, sound, or gesture/posture. Make sure you can repeat the anchor exactly.

Kinesthetic anchors: be able to repeat in exact location with same pressure.

Visual or auditory anchors: choose a gesture, body posture, word, or sound you can repeat exactly but do not use habitually. An alternative visual or auditory anchor is respectfully using the person's own word, tone, or gesture to re-access a particular state.

d. Test the anchor when the person is in a neutral state. If you do not calibrate the anchored response, elicit response again, anchor again and re-test. **Or** strengthen anchor by stacking or using submodalities.

Stacking Anchors: connecting several experiences of the same response to one anchor. For example, accessing three experiences of confidence, having person relive each and anchoring him/her on the same spot or with the same gesture or word/sound.

Submodalities: identify the submodality which intensifies the response when either increased or decreased. For example, making a picture brighter or longer, or a voice louder or faster and anchoring the intensified response.

Visual And Auditory Anchoring

1. Pick out three distinctive but neutral gestures or body positions which you can do easily but don't do habitually, **or** pick out three sounds or words that you can repeat exactly but don't do habitually.

2. During an interaction, notice when a person is in a positive emotional state (facial animation, voice, body movement, etc.). While the person is in that state, repeat one element in Step #1—gesture, body position, sound or word. Each time that state comes up again, repeat the anchor three or four times.

3. When the person is in a neutral state, test the anchor by making that gesture, body position, sound or saying the word, and notice how strongly you elicit that same emotional state (calibrate).

4. Use the anchors you have established whenever appropriate to the situation and outcome.

Note: This process can be enhanced by identifying the person's own self-anchors. Often the person will make a particular gesture, adopt a certain body position, make a particular sound, or use certain words when in a specific emotional state. When repeated in a respectful manner by the communicator, these anchors will retrigger that positive state.

Future Pacing

The process of associating a specific response (emotion, cognitive process, skill) to a specific future situation.

Process

1. Identify and access desired response (resource).
2. Anchor response.
3. Identify specific context and/or **trigger** (what you see/hear just before needing the resource).
4. Fire off anchor and see/hear trigger/context simultaneously. Do this 3 to 5 times.
5. Test: see/hear trigger/context without anchor.

Note: The result of successful **Future-Pacing** is that the context or stimulus automatically triggers the desired response.

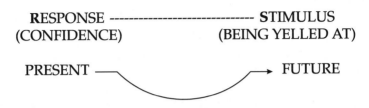

Self-Anchoring

The creation of an association between a stimulus and a desired response, when the person him/herself deliberately creates both the stimulus and the desired response.

The stimulus can be a unique gesture or touch (i.e., holding thumb and forefinger together or touching an ear lobe) or a specific word or shift in posture. This is connected through repetition to a pre-determined response.

Procedure

1. Identify what response you want and in what situation you want it. For example, you may want to be more confident with your boss.

2. Pick a unique and simple gesture, touch, or posture. **Note:** It is necessary that the stimulus be unique and not something you do often, or else it will become associated with many responses and lose its potency.

3. Remember a situation in your life when you strongly experienced the desired response. Usually this is more easily identified in a **different** context from the one in which you want it. For example, instead of trying to remember a time when you were confident with your boss, remember when you felt confident with your customers, friends, etc.

4. Re-live this experience as fully as possible **and** hold or do your pre-identified stimulus (anchor) for at least 10 seconds. Repeat this 3 times.

5. Clear your experience by taking a deep breath and changing your posture. Do your anchor. Wait several seconds. You will experience the desired response. If you do not, repeat Step 4.

Note: If you want to make the response stronger, re-live **several** past experiences of the desired response while holding the anchor.

You now have created a Self-Anchor that you can use anytime when it would be useful for you to have the anchored response. It will continue to work until an association is automatically made between that particular situation and the desired response. It can only be extinguished by an unexpected and much stronger response.

As-If Frame
Derived from the work of Richard Bandler and John Grinder

Frames establish and maintain the boundaries of exploration. They define the precise process you are doing. This helps the communicator to stay on track and make the essential distinction between the **need to know** and the **need not to know**—that is, what information is important to pursue in order to reach your outcome and what information is not necessary.

As If Frame

This process enables you to gather information that is ordinarily unavailable. It asks the person to suspend judgement and reality, and **act as if** he/she had achieved some desired outcome. You're shifting his/her perspective and gathering information from "contrary-to-fact" situation.

Technique

1. Ask person to **Act As If** . . .
From that perspective, ask what he/she sees, hears, feels, how it affects his/her life, behavior, emotions.

2. Ask person to **Act As If** it is sometime in the future (week, month, year) and he/she has reached some important outcome. Once you have shifted the person into the future, be sure to use **present tense verbs**; i.e., you **are**, how **is** it affecting you, how others **are** responding.

You can use descriptions of weather, holidays, etc. that are congruent with where in the future you have brought the person; i.e., if it is February, talk about the cold and wearing warm clothes, December, you might talk about the holidays, May, you could talk about the warm air and flowers blossoming.

3. From this perspective, explore with person what he/she sees, hears, feels, how it affects his/her work, family, health, what it feels like to enjoy this achievement. You could also explore **how** he/she reached this outcome.

    a. Use the following lead-in phrases:
       • **Act As If**...
       • Let's suppose that...
       • Pretend that...
       • If you were to...
    b. Types of **As If:**
       •Time (going into future, pretend it's six months from now and...)
       •Person (if you were me or someone else...)
       •Information (let's suppose that you need that information...)
       •Behavior (**act as if** you could do that, what...)

Uses

1.   To increase the flow of information when it is difficult to gather it in the ordinary way.

2.   To check **Ecology**.

3.   To motivate the person.

4.   To overcome discouragement by creating the experience of the possibility of a outcome.

Beliefs

Beliefs help to organize one's life, and **Criteria** provide the glue of coherency.

A Belief is a Generalization we have made about ourselves and/or the world that we are convinced is true. Beliefs are organized around values and are usually rules about how to achieve or avoid important values.

Beliefs drive our behavior and are mostly unconscious. We do not question our need for oxygen; we have a similar attitude toward our beliefs. "Whoever discovered water—you can be sure it was not the fish." We are in a similar situation in relation to our beliefs. We don't think very much about them and are rarely conscious of them until they are brought to our attention.

A **Generalization:**   a rule that defines the relationship between/among experiences or parts of experience.

A **Criterion:**   a value that provides the basis or standard upon which people evaluate experience. Criteria are values around which people organize beliefs.

An **Assumption:**	something we assume to be true, take for granted. **Example:** I assume that when I switch on my lights, they will go on.
Beliefs and Assumptions:	the same except beliefs have a much stronger and wider impact on a person's life, often going across several or all contexts (large generalizations).
Beliefs:	personal, significant, and compelling in one's life, and organized around an important value (criterion).
Assumptions:	trivial and/or not personally compelling, and usually **not** organized around an important value.

Beliefs are held strong and constant by the person's particular filters, the subjective experience of the achievement or avoidance of highly valued criteria that reinforce the belief, and the ability to delete or distort experiences that would be counter-examples to the belief. This is accomplished by the person's individual constellation of meta program patterns and his/her Complex Equivalence of Criteria.

Five Different Levels of Beliefs:
Derived from the work of Robert Dilts

1.	**Environment**	**Where/When (e.g., "I can't concentrate in a messy room")**
2.	**Behavior**	**What (e.g., "I'm clumsy")**
3.	**Capability**	**How (e.g., "I never get it right")**
4.	**Values**	**Why (e.g., "I have to be strong")**
5.	**Identity**	**Who (e.g., "I am what I do," "I'm not lovable")**

Identifying Beliefs
Based on the work of Anné Linden

Identifying Beliefs in General

1. Ask person,"What do you have to believe in order to do, say, feel, or believe that?" Keep asking this question until you get the significant underlying belief.

2. Listen to the words (surface structure) and ask yourself, "What does this person have to assume is true in order to make this/ these statements?" Then feedback what you think it is—calibrate and remember to respect the other's model of the world. This is an interactive process—you must be willing to be wrong! You must also be willing to go back and forth refining the belief.

Feedback what you think are the primary beliefs—interact with the person until it "clicks" with him/her. Calibrate—there will be a significant response when you identify the underlying belief. Remember, people are not conscious of their beliefs, and the process of identifying a belief is that of bringing the belief to conscious awareness.

Specific Approaches to Identify Old Limiting Beliefs

Person identifies context where he/she is limited (where he/ she has an impasse, a problem, or an outcome he/she is not achieving) **or context within which he/she wants to be different but is not.**

1. **Within this context, complete the sentences in 1, 2 and 3:**
    a. It's important for people to_____.
    b. It's wrong for people to_____.
    c. People should_____.

2. a. Describe a success and a failure.
    b. Describe a behavior that you label as a limitation.
    c. Describe how you motivate self.

d. Describe how you accomplish goals and overcome obstacles.
e. Describe how you evaluate and appreciate self.

3. a. How do you want to be different?
    b. What stops you?
    c. What do you want? What do you have?
    d. Who are you? Who should you be? Who do you want to be?

Note: It is important to stay in the same context with all these examples and/or questions.

Either:

1. Ask what do you have to believe in order to _____ ?
   or:
2. Listen and identify what it is this person is assuming to be true about themselves and the world without actually saying it. In either case, feed back what you think the belief is and interact until it "clicks"—and you've identified the underlying belief.

Categories of Beliefs & Some Sample Beliefs

Categories

Categories organized according to the five levels:

1. **Environment**
2. **Behavior**
3. **Capabilities**
4. **Values**
5. **Identity**

Other Categories:

1.	**Either/Or**	I can be smart or emotional. I can be successful or a good parent. I can be independent or have a relationship.
2.	**Being Enough**	I'm not enough. I'm not smart enough, clever enough, good looking enough, thin enough.
3.	**Being Deserving**	I don't deserve—to succeed, to be loved, etc.
4.	**Comparisons (Others & Self)**	Others are better than me.
5.	**Self/Other Needs**	Others have to be happy so than I can be loved.
6.	**Worth/Identity (Determined By What Person Does)**	I am what I do/what I accomplish.
7.	**Lovableness**	I am/not lovable.
8.	**All or Nothing**	It/I must be perfect or it isn't worthwhile.

Some Sample Beliefs

I'm ugly, stupid.
Others have to get what they want before I can get what I want.
I can be smart and emotional or I can be smart **or** emotional.
I can feel **and** get what I want or I can feel **or** get what I want.
Feelings are dangerous friends.
Others have to be happy so that I can be loved.
I can be separate **or** connect with others.

I can be separate **and** connect with others.
I am what I do/accomplish.
I am in charge of my life.
Others are in charge of my life.
World is a dangerous place.
I need a relationship to be fulfilled/successful, etc.
Alone is failure.
I have to do it if it's going to be done right.
Change takes time/No one/Nothing ever changes.
Unless I'm _____, I'm nothing.
I am run by my feelings.
I get better every year.
I can either think or react.

I'm not lovable.
Life is over at 30-40-60, etc.
Nothing lasts.
Struggle is necessary—one must struggle.
If it's easy it's not worthwhile.

I'm nobody.
I don't deserve success love, etc.
I have to get sick to get attention.
I have to get/do it all or it doesn't count.
Anything less than everything is failure.

Compromise is failure.
I can take care of myself no matter how I feel.
I'm invisible.
I don't deserve to exist.
I'm not going to live.

I can be visible with impact.
It's not safe to be visible.
My life is blessed.
I'm valuable. I have the right to express myself.
I can't change.
I'm loving and lovable.
I don't count.

I can only be who I am when I'm alone.
Being sick gets me attention.
I have the right to be alive.
Safety is in anonymity.
Being visible is dangerous.
I create my own specialness.
I am worthless.
I am powerful.
I am the source of my own creation.

Reimprinting Process I
Based on the work of Robert Dilts

1. **Establish in general terms** where present, past, and future **Time Line** is. Have person step into a spot on floor that represents present, and then look at future and past as represented by lines on the floor.

2. **Have person get into Internal State of old belief** and step on present in his/her time line.

3. **Keeping that Internal State, have person walk backwards** on his/her past Time Line until she/he gets to the **first** time she/he had this Internal State—this impasse. This will be the experience that imprinted the belief.

4. **Have person step backwards on his/her past Time Line** to **before** s/he had this belief. Experience self without this belief.

5. **Have person step off his/her Time Line.** Look at imprinting experience. Identify positive intent of responses—your own and others' in the experience. Identify resources needed in that imprinting experience.

6. **Step on Time Line where person experiences** the resources. Self-anchor.

7. **Step on Time Line just before imprinting experience**—hold

self-anchor and step into initial imprint. Relive this experience with resource.

8. **Walk along the Time Line to the present experiencing** reimprinting. Use references or other resources if necessary.

9. **Return to present and verbalize new/updated belief.** Is it the same as new belief person previously decided upon?

Reimprinting II For Self Esteem
Based on the work of Anné Linden

1. Subject identifies either a belief or an emotion that is damaging to **self-esteem**.

2. Establish in general terms where present, past, and future **Time Line** is. Have subject step onto a spot on floor that represents **present** and look at **future** and **past** as if represented by lines in the floor.

3. Ask subject to get inside the limiting emotion or belief—experience it now as fully as possible. Subject is standing in **present**.

4. Instruct subject to maintain that experience and that you (Guide) will guide them as he/she begins to slowly walk backward on his/her past until he/she gets to the **first time** he/she ever had this emotion or belief. Suggest to subject that he/she can allow his/her unconscious mind to guide him/her to this memory—"the first time you ever experienced this emotion or belief." This will be the experience that imprinted the belief.

5. Subject will stop once he/she reaches that experience. Instruct subject to take 2 steps backwards to **before** that experience ever happened. Encourage subject to fully experience and feel him/herself without that emotion/belief.

6. Have subject step off his/her **Time Line**. Look at and listen to

Self in that imprinting experience. Maintain boundaries (can step into Fair Witness position). From this perspective, identify how subject (younger self) was doing best he/she could under the circumstances.

7. Subject steps back onto **Time Line** just **before** imprinting experience. Subject establishes peripheral vision and hearing—boundaries. If necessary, hold fingers up to each side, representing peripheral seeing.

Note: In case of extreme trauma subject can put a translucent bubble around self—he/she can see and hear through this bubble. However, the bubble separates and protects subject as he/she moves through the imprinting experience. While maintaining peripheral vision, subject experiences in body what it's like to be in the world without that limiting emotion/belief.

8. Subject maintains peripheral vision/hearing (with fingers or bubble) and bodily sensation of being in world without the limiting emotion/belief and other new awarenesses *and* steps forward on **Time Line** into imprinting experience. Have subject continue to move through experience; reliving it with boundaries and new awareness.

9. Subject continues to walk along **Time Line** toward **present**—maintaining peripheral vision, etc. Suggest to subject as he/she moves along to "Allow other experiences to shift or adjust according to whatever changes occurred for you during the reimprinting." "Allow other experiences to shift as they will—appropriately for now." "You don't have to understand this—your unconscious can do this." Keep subject moving—do this relatively quickly.

10. Subject returns to present. From this perspective ask, "What is your experience **now** of that emotion/belief you **had**?" "What new learnings are you **now** aware of?"

Have subject look to his/her **future** and imagine self moving into **future** with these new learnings. Appreciate ability to evolve, and see self as an evolving process.

Transforming Old Belief Into New Belief
Based on the work of Richard Bandler

Submodality Belief Process

1. **Identify how person represents** (internally—submodalities) the old belief.

2. **Have person identify something he/she is in doubt about.** Identify how person represents this (submodalities).

3. **Use contrast frame to elicit the differences in the submodalities** between old belief and doubt. Identify the most impactful submodalities of doubt. (They will be represented in different spatial locations.)

4. **Give the old belief the submodalities of the doubt.** Start with the most impactful submodality. This also means moving the representation of the old belief to the spatial location of the doubt. Have person practice several times, representing the old belief with the submodalities of the doubt, until he/she represents it only this way.

5.**Identify a belief person has and likes.** This is **not** the new belief—simply another useful belief. Identify the submodalities of this belief. Contrast these with submodalities of doubt. Identify what submodalities make this belief more certain. Put this information aside for future use.

6. **Represent the now doubtful belief (now with submodalities of doubt).** Close a door on this belief—**hear** it close and see on the front of the closed door a picture of the new belief. (Submodalities are not important here.)

7. **Take this picture and move it quickly to the horizon**—so that it becomes a tiny spot. Then bring it back with all the

impactful submodalities of the belief person has and likes—the submodalities make the belief more certain (Step 5) Do this several times if necessary to install the new belief.

8. **Test: Ask person to think of new belief.** Calibrate where he/she is accessing and other responses. Check that new belief is now automatically represented with submodalities of Step 5.

Summary of Submodality Shifts

1. In this diagram the submodalities are represented as a rectangle and a square.

   A.

   | old belief | | doubt |

   Contrast Submodalities of old belief and doubt

2. Remember to keep separate content and form— the submodalities

   B.

   | | old belief |

   Give old belief submodalities of doubt

   C.
   Identify submodalities of belief person likes

   | | belief |

   D.
   Give new belief submodalities of belief person likes.

   | | new belief |

Change History
Based on the work of Richard Bandler and John Grinder

This process can be used to help someone change his/her perspective and attitude about past experiences that support undesirable and limiting feelings in the present. It doesn't change the events themselves, but does significantly change a person's beliefs about self relating to these past experiences.

Procedure

• **Part One**

1. **Ask client to identify a feeling** that has occurred over time which is unwanted and which limits him/her. Calibrate that the client has fully accessed the feeling and **anchor**.

2. **Hold this anchor and ask client to go back through time and space** (as though each year were a page in a scrapbook of his/her life and he/she is turning the pages backwards), allowing her unconscious mind to identify past experiences that have the same or similar feeling. (These memories need not make logical sense.)

3. **Ask client to verbally label** each experience (briefly).

4. **After 3-5 experiences have been identified** and named, **release anchor**. Bring client back to here and now.

• **Part Two**

1. **Ask client to identify a resource** that would help younger self in those past experiences to **feel okay about self**.

2. **Ask client to access experiences of this resource** in his/her life and **anchor**. If necessary, access and ANCHOR (in different places) two different resources.

3. **Hold the resource anchor, take the client back through each experience in Part One** so that he/she can get through each experience feeling okay about him/herself. He/she can change what he/she did or not, whatever is necessary in order to go through the experience **with** the present resource **and** feel okay about self. **Constraint:** Person **cannot** change other people or external events in the experience.

4. **Release resource anchors.** Bring client back to here and now.

• **Part Three**

1. **Testing: Ask the client to review Part One** experiences without **anchors. Calibrate** response to see if there is a change.

2. **Testing: ask the client to think of a recent example** of this undesirable feeling. **Calibrate** to see if the resource is working. If not, use **anchor** to get client through experience and feel okay about himself.

3. **Testing: ask the client to go into the future** and imagine a situation in which he/she would ordinarily experience the old undesirable feeling. **Calibrate.**

If the client has any trouble **feeling okay about self and experiencing options,** ask him/her to identify an external stimulus that immediately precedes the old undesirable feeling **(the trigger). Anchor** the resource to that stimulus. Do this 2 or 3 times.

Test again—if necessary test with worst possible situation in an imagined future.

Comparisons
Self-to-Idealized-Self Comparison Process
Based on the work of Anné Linden

1. **Elicit how the person knows the difference between the**

present and the future, with the emphasis on how he/she represents the future. Identify the submodalities that let the person know that something will happen in the near, middle and far future. Ask him/her to make an image of something he/she knows will happen tomorrow, a month from now, a year from now. Elicit the differences in each in terms of submodalities:

a. Spacial—this includes the location of the image in space, which can be easily determined by having the person point to where his/her visual representation of a particular time is located, and the distance from the person
b. size
c. brightness—light/dark
d. dimensionality—2-dimensional, 3-dimensional
e. color/black & white—intensity: primary, pastel, muted
f. focus—clarity/fuzziness
g. opaqueness/translucent/transparent

For some individuals other submodalities may be more relevant. However, I have found that generally people code time with one or more of the above. It is essential that you elicit the idiosyncratic submodalities that determine the specific time frame. It usually includes the spacial submodality.

2. **Determine in what context** the "I should already . . ." occurs. The self-to-idealized-self comparison with negative results.

3. **Elicit the image of self that the person is using** (if this is out-of-conscious awareness and represented by a feeling, ask the person to imagine an image of Self that would represent that feeling) as the measurement of success or achievement.

4. **Get the person to appreciate his/her ideal self** and determine where in the future this image would be realistic and ecological for the specific situation and context.

5. **Change the submodalities of the idealized self-image** to those that represent that place in time that is most ecological for that

person. For example, if the comparison works best when the ideal self is represented a year from now, you give that image the submodality characteristics that code it for the person as a year in the future. Rehearse these changes so that they are installed and automatically associated with that particular image.

> Be alert for any objections: This is how you will know where in the future to put the ideal image. Also, you may have to reassure the person that he or she is not losing or giving up any ideals; rather, the therapist is ensuring that he or she have a more positive attitude and motivation that will assist him/her in coming closer and closer to this ideal.

6. First, **test your work by asking the person to access the idealized image**—making sure that he or she always represents it with the appropriate future submodalities. Next, **test the ecology in the particular context**. Associate the person to that context and have him/her go through a future situation. Calibrate. Ask the person for feedback.

7. **After determining that this shift is ecological and there are no objections**, future pace to other possible situations.

Note: Issues of ecology and objections sometimes relate to where in the future the idealized self-image is placed, or to fear of giving up an ideal.

Self-To-Other Comparison Process
Based on the work of Anné Linden

I can't/I haven't got/I should have—change to—**I want/(I can)/ I will**

1. Identify context (specific event and person).

2. **What do I want that the other person has or does?**
    What is it about the person that I covet/lust after: behavior/ skill/attitude/possessions, etc.
    Identify what is wanted—what you wish you had.

3. **What will this do for me?—(outcome sequitor)**

4. **Is this ecological? Is it possible? (Ecology/Reality check)**
   If yes: continue. **If no**: chunk down—to what **is** realistic or go back to Step 3 and find another, more ecological way to satisfy this.

5. • **Make movie of person doing it (X).**
   • **Substitute Self—watch and listen.**
   • **Step inside—check out how it (X) feels.**

6. • **Do I still want it (X)? Identify scenario/strategy to achieve X.**
   Chunk down the steps necessary to achieve your outcome.
   If yes: What do I have to do to get this (X)? How can I learn this? Do this?
   If no: Exit and do something else.

7. **Is it worth it?**
   If no: What part of it would be worthwhile? (Do the same as if yes.) **OR**
   It's not worth it to me—Exit and do something else.

   If yes: What's the first step, and when will I do it? Make this specific and concrete.

Note: Keep the image of you having what you want in order to motivate yourself.

Criteria
Based on the work of Richard Bandler and John Grinder

"A cognitive organism evaluates its experience and because it evaluates them it tends to repeat certain ones and avoid others."
—Ernst von Glaserfeld

Criteria are the values that give meaning to people's experience and provide the structure that creates in us the desire to repeat or avoid those experiences. **Criteria** are the standards we use to evaluate our experiences. As infants, we begin life with two basic criteria: Survival (in the form of Safety/Danger) and Pleasure/Pain. As we grow, learn and mature we expand and define these basic values as a result of experience. A criterion always has two sides: that which is desired and that which is to be avoided; what we move toward and what we move away from; e.g., Creative/Mechanical, Beauty/Ugliness, Responsible/Irresponsible. Be careful about assuming what the opposite criterion is—this is very idiosyncratic. When you've identified an important criterion, ask, "What is the inverse or opposite of that?"

Criteria	the values around which we organize our Beliefs.
Beliefs	generalizations or rules about ourselves and/or the world that enable us to achieve or avoid a highly valued criterion.
Generalizations	rules that define the relationship between or among experiences or pieces of experience.
Presupposition	a linguistic reflection of a belief.
Criteria	are usually expressed as **nominalizations**; e.g., Fairness, Responsibility, Uniqueness, Creativity, Freedom, Perseverance, Warmth, Responsiveness, Boredom, Inefficiency, Tension, Immobility, Wastefulness, etc. Each of these has its complementary opposite.
Detection of Criteria	The word (nominalization) or phrase representing the criterion is marked out or emphasized by:
1. **Repetition**	criterion is repeated a number of times; based on number of times used.

2. **Intensity**	indicated by facial expression, gesture, shift in pitch, tempo, volume, etc.
3. **Frequency**	repetition based not on number of times used but how close together it is used.
4. **Difference**	indicated by a shift in external behavior from the "normal" behavior.

Elicitation of Criteria

When a person is using descriptions of behavior, generalizations or words that describe emotions rather than nominalizations, then it is necessary to ask questions:

Questions Useful in Eliciting the Criterion:

- "What about **that** is important to you?" or "How is that important?"
- "What does **that** accomplish for you?"
- "What does **that** do for you?"
- "Of what value is **that** to you?"

e.g.:

- "When I'm able to **see all the pieces** and **know how and when I'm going to use them,** I feel good."
- "What does that accomplish for you?"
- "It means I'm organized."

The first sentence is a **description of behavior**; the question elicited the criterion of **organization**.

- "I'm **feeling** very **concerned** and **worried** about her."
- "How is that important to you?"
- "Because I'm very **connected** to her."

The first sentence describes **emotions**; the question elicited the criterion of **connection**.

Utilization of Criteria

These skills affect people's experience of their values, thereby increasing choices. There are basically two categories of criteria utilization:

1. **Utilization of the Word** (nominalization) itself—without necessarily knowing the specific meaning of the word to the person using it.

> a. **Match**: A criterion can be considered a **key word**. Use this word to increase rapport.
> b. **Hierarchy**: Identifying a more important criterion and using it. (See Eliciting Criteria Hierarchy, pg. 159.)
> c. **Spin**: This is creating a paradoxical situation for the person by putting him/her in between satisfying one criterion and violating another. (See **SPIN**, pg. 160)
> d. **Criterion Re-Prioritizing**: Using Submodalities to change the importance of a particular criterion—making it either more or less important. (See Re-Prioritization of Criterion, pg. 163)

2. **Eliciting the Complex Equivalence of a criterion**—the sensory-based definition or description of the word/nominalization representing the criterion. For example, when **attention** is an important criterion to a person eliciting the specific idiosyncratic description/meaning of that criterion. How does he/she know someone is paying **attention** to him/her? When the other person looks at him, touches her, repeats her words, etc. And how does he/she pay attention to someone else?

In identifying the **Complex Equivalence,** you are finding what **must** be in an experience; either the fulfillment and avoidance of the criteria.

Questions to elicit Complex Equivalence

> a. How do you experience?

b. How do you know?

c. What do you see and hear?

Using a criterion in this way demands that you discover first the meaning or **Complex Equivalence** of the criterion and **then** expand, adjust or change that meaning by creating a **Counter-Example** to that definition/meaning:

a. **Shift Perceptual Positions**: Change Point of View— Identify someone the person respects who has same criterion but a different Complex Equivalence.

b. **Identify a Time** when the **Complex Equivalence** was different, but still represented the criterion.

c. **Contrast two situations** that have the same criterion but different **Complex Equivalences**.

d. **Change Time Frame and/or Context**: How will this apply 10 years from now, or in a business context, or on Mars.

e. **Re-Define the Meaning**: Give the **Complex Equivalence** another label rather than the value/criterion used by the person.

f. **Use of Universals**: "It's always going to be. . . ." "It never could be different. . . ."

g. **Use As If Frame**

Counter-Examples

The ability to elicit or create a counter-example is fundamental to the art of persuasion and change. Resources are hidden in counter-examples.

A **Counter-Example** is an experience that matches, is similar to or the same as another or other experiences with some significant differences. For example, a man who is confident about himself except when with people who are much older than him.

Two types of Counter-Examples are:

1. When the situation is the same but the response is different; person is paying attention to something else. For example, a woman is able to be patient with children except right after she returns home from work. A boy is allergic to cats except his best friend's cat.

Foreground/Background Phenomena: When you see two triangles, for example, how do you make one more important than the other?

2. When the situation is **similar** and response is **different**. The person has a different response in a situation that is not the same but is similar enough to be considered in the same category as initial situation—by chunking UP or laterally. For example, a woman always gets depressed when her children fight—a **similar** but not the same situation might be when her colleagues or friends fight, and she does not get depressed. A woman gets seasick on a boat when she is not driving it—a **similar** situation is when she is riding in a bus or subway, and she does not get sick.

Note: Important that the subject accept that the **similar** situation is connected to original situation—and could be considered the same even though technically it is not.

Ways to Elicit Counter-Examples

1. **Change Context**
2. **Change Perspective**: shift perceptual positions
3. **Change Time Frame**
4. **Contrast** two situations that are either different and identify similarities, or two situations that are similar and identify differences.

5. **Re-define** or **Reframe** the meaning of a situation
6. Use **As If Frame**
7. **Play Polarity**
8. **Use** of **Universal Quantifiers**, "It's always been . . . ?" "There has never been . . . ?" "Has there ever been a time . . . ?"

Questions To Elicit The Criteria Ladder (Hierarchy)
Derived from the work of Richard Bandler and Leslie Cameron-Bandler

Example: Someone wants to be better at small talk with people.

1. **First elicit the criterion which is stopping the person.** This is the basis of the ladder, and in general, will be first rung on the ladder. Questions like: "What stops you from making small talk . . . ?, or How does it serve you *not* to make small talk . . . ?" will usually get the criterion. In the small talk example below, the answer was **Privacy.**

CRITERIA

	TOWARD	AWAY	
T3	Connection	Alienation	A3
T2	Creativity	Boredom	A2
T1	Privacy	Exposure	A1

2. **Privacy** is only one side of the **complete** criterion for that person. In order to get its opposite or counterpart, a couple of possible questions are:

a. What's the opposite/(flip side) of **Privacy**?
b. If **Privacy** were violated, what would you have?

3. You can move up the criteria ladder on either the **Toward** or

the **Away From** side. Once you get either side of the next higher rung, you can then get its opposite. The form of the question for moving up the ladder is:

TOWARD

What would have to exist for you to . . . move away from **Privacy**

What would make it necessary for you to . . . give up **Privacy**

What would be important enough for you to . . . subordinate **Privacy**

What would get (force) you to . . . suspend, let go of **Privacy**

What would have to happen for you to . . . ignore, override, overrule **Privacy**

What would make you give up . . . overlook **Privacy**

AWAY FROM

What would have to exist for you to . . . endure, tolerate **Exposure**

What would be important enough for you to . . . continue, deal with **Exposure**

What would get (force) you to . . . subject yourself to **Exposure**

What would have to happen for you to . . . move toward, approach **Exposure**

What would make you give up . . . wallow in, stay with, experience **Exposure**

The "Spin"
Derived from the work of Richard Bandler, Anné Linden and Dean Taylor

Example: Subject wants to be able to engage in **Small Talk** at social gatherings, but cannot. **The Ladder Has Been Elicited** (see below). In general, the idea is to create a conflict between two criteria. The first rung, **Privacy (T1)—(T—toward, A—away) Exposure (A—1)**, is the criterion which stops the person from doing X, in this case **Small Talk. The general rule of the spin is: In order to continue what you're doing (i.e., satisfy the first**

criteria level—Not make Small Talk), you are violating a more highly valued criterion (level 3).

CRITERIA

TOWARD	AWAY
Connection	Alienation
Creativity	Boredom
Privacy	Exposure

1. To put a person between **T1 (Privacy)** and **A3 (Alienation)**, the question has the person going **Toward** or **Getting** both . . . To get privacy, you also get alienation.

"Is your **Privacy** so important that you are willing to be **Alienated?**"
"Are you willing to feel **Alienation** in order to maintain your **Privacy?**"

2. To put a person between **A1 (Exposure)** and **T3 (Connection)**, your question has the person **Not Getting** either (going **Away From** both).

"Is preventing your **Exposure** so important that you're willing to give up feeling **Connected?**"
"So you're willing to not feel **Connected** just so that you won't be **Exposed?**"

3. To **Spin** a person on the same side, your question allows the person to **Get** the first level criterion **(T1—A1)**, but **Not Get** the higher level criterion **(T3-A3)**, i.e., going **Toward** one and **Away From** the other.

Toward side: "You mean you're willing to sacrifice **Connectedness** just to maintain your sense of **Privacy?**"

"Is **Privacy** so important that you'll give up your **Connect-edness** just to maintain your sense of **Privacy?**"

Away side: "Are you willing to feel **Alienated** simply to keep from feeling **Exposed**?"

"Is preventing **Exposure** so important that you're willing to feel **Alienation**?"

Remember, this is just one format; this is not the **only** way to generate a **Spin**. If what you're doing isn't working, Try Something Else!

Re-Prioritization Of Criterion
Based on the work of Richard Bandler

1. **Identify a criterion** the person wants to make more or less important. Check ecology.

2. **Identify three levels of the person's criteria ladder—not** the criterion the person wants to make more or less important. (See Elicitation of **Criteria Hierarchy**.)

3. **Identify the analogue submodalities** that code the relative importance of these three criteria. It is usually best to use the **Toward** criteria—although you can use the **Away** criteria. In either case you **must** use three criteria that are the **same** direction.

Analogue Submodalities are on a continuum—small to large, clear to fuzzy, etc.; rather than digital: either/or, color or black and white, framed or panoramic, etc.

Ask the person to represent all **three** criteria visually and simultaneously. Ask how he/she knows which is more/or less important. You can do this **Auditorally** also. (Using **Primary Kinesthetic** Submodalities is possible but more difficult.)

Identify two or three Analogue Submodalities that enable the person to know the relative importance of the three criteria: which one is most important, least important, and in between. This step is solely for the purpose of identifying these submodalities; the criteria you use to do this has nothing to do with the **Re-Prioritization Process**.

4. Take criterion A that the person wants to make more (or less) important, and then establish what other criterion B the person wants A to be more (or less) important than.

5. **Using criterion B as a reference point,** direct the person to choose the **Relevant Submodalities** of **Criterion A**. That criterion is more or less important than **Criterion B**. Do this slowly. For example, if the submodalities that code a person's criteria hierarchy are size, distance and color intensity (where larger, closer and increased intensity equals more importance and the opposite equals decreased importance), you would have the person increase the size and color intensity of **Criterion A** and move it closer until it was larger, closer and had more color intensity than **Criterion B**.

Re-Prioritization of Criteria

Slowly make the image of **Criterion A** larger; increase the intensity of the color and move it closer than **Criterion B**.

6. **Have person do this until** he/she finds where the changed submodalities "feel right." Have him/her "click" it into place. Be alert for any objections and deal with them immediately.

7. **Test Future-Pace:**

   a. Ask person to think of **Criterion A**. The image that comes to mind should automatically be represented with the changed submodalities; i.e., larger, smaller, closer, farther, etc.
   b. Put person into situation where the re-prioritized criterion would make a difference. Have the person associate to this situation and live it. Calibrate, get feedback from the person.

Expectations
Based on the work of Anné Linden

If you want to change or adjust your expectations, the following technique is useful. (You can do this on yourself, but with difficult situations or for the first time it's more useful for someone else to guide you through it and do the anchoring.) Assist person to:

1. **Identify a situation of continuous disappointment or frustration**—or another type of situation in which your expectations are not helpful and yet you keep having them.

2. **Identify what actually happens in this situation.**

> **Identify your expectations.** Take time to completely separate the reality of the situation from your expectations. **Make a detailed, multi-sensory movie of each.** Represent both from beginning to end. If you think you can't do this, pretend—make it up.

3. **Do the following with each**—the movie of what actually happens **and** the movie of your expectations. You are going to watch each movie several times, each time changing one aspect of it. After each change return your movie to "normal"; the way you originally represented it, then change another aspect and run the movie again.

> a. **Identify whether you are seeing yourself (dissociated) or whether you are seeing through your eyes inside the experience (associated).**
> Watch the movie again only this time watch from a different perspective; i.e. if you were dissociated originally—seeing yourself, this time be associated; and if originally associated, this time be dissociated—seeing yourself. Do this once through from beginning to end.
> b. **Watch the movie again** as you represented it originally, but this time slow it down to a third the original speed.

Watch it again and speed it up 3 to 4 times as fast as originally represented.

c. **Watch it again**, this time through the eyes of someone else
or, if no one else was involved, through the "eyes" of an
object in the movie.

4. **Ask self "Given what actually happens is it worth it to have
that expectation that way?"** "Do I want to continue to have that
particular expectation?"

If answer is **no**, go to the next step.
If answer is **yes**, identify the objections and take care of them.
You may decide you want to continue as before.

5.   **Anchor (A) the expectation**—test to make sure you have an
anchor.
Anchor (B) what actually happens—test to make sure you
have an **anchor**.
Collapse anchors A and B.

6. **Develop a new and more useful expectation**: one that is more
worthwhile (given the reality of the situation) and that retains
what is important for you and your values. Changing your
expectations does **not** mean giving up your values. See yourself
in your new expectation and use other submodalities in the visual
and auditory systems to make the representation of the new
expectation more detailed, concrete, positively impactful and
realistic.

Create a multi-sensory movie of the new expectation.

7. **Picture and hear** the new expectation and then the old
expectation. Compare them. Pick which one you'd rather have—
given what actually happens.

If you want the old expectation, go back to Step 4.
If you choose the new expectation, step inside your
representation of it (Associate). Check out the ecology and
refine realistically to your satisfaction. Anchor this (C).

8. **Dissociate—see self in new expectation.** Identify a future situation where you want to have this new expectation.

Identify the trigger for the old expectation. "What was it you saw and/or heard just before you got disappointed or frustrated?" See and/or hear this in your mind's eye and, as you do, fire off Anchor C. Do this several times. (Future-pace.)

9. **Test: "Re-live"** a future experience of that same disappointment or frustration you identified in Step 1. What is your experience of that now? Does the new expectation click in automatically? If not, check ecology and go back to Step 8.

Note: One of the most important steps in this technique is Step 2—separating what actually happens from the expectation.

In intensely felt situations, the "reality," or what actually happens, and our expectations are usually enmeshed and at first seem as though they're the same. Sometimes it is enough simply to separate these to realize how limiting our expectation is and to want to change it. In separating the expectation and reality, you are bringing to conscious awareness what it is specifically you've been expecting and can decide if it is realistic or helpful. Especially in relationship to what "actually happens." Once you have clearly and solidly separated them as two distinct experiences there is value in then collapsing them. This process helps you to use the information contained in the "reality experience" with that represented by the "expectation" to build a new expectation. This collapsing of two separate experiences is very different than having one experience that muddles reality with what you want.

Consider what your expectations are about yourself and others in various situations. How are your feelings of trust, appreciation, success, and love affected by your expectations? Have they been helpful in achieving your goals and becoming more of who you want to be? If so, reinforce them; if not, you might change them!

Fair Witness
Based on the work of Anné Linden

This position embodies non-polar thinking (no good/bad, right/ wrong), simply being totally present and available with no need to help, fix, judge, or change. The key to this is **Acceptance**. Not in the sense of approval or loving, but simply acceptance of what *is.* The **Fair Witness Position** facilitates non-judgmental observations and information-gathering while generating an active presence that creates a safe, non-evaluating environment.

The **Witness** is very involved in interacting and talking with the other, giving him/her an opportunity to express herself, talk about him/herself, her life, dreams, fears, hopes, madness, sanity—whatever is relevant to the moment and the person. The **Fair Witness** connects and identifies with the other's experience and emotions, allowing one's self to be moved and affected by the other **and** maintaining separation, that is, maintains boundaries.

Fundamental to this position is **"Not Caring."** This means letting go of all need or desire to help or fix—having no investment in the other person changing, feeling better, more comfortable, happier, solving a problem or achieving a desired goal. **"Not Caring"** does **not** mean not caring about the humanity of the other or being detached and aloof. It combines acceptance of what **is** with no need to **change** it, and active involvement with the other person—being affected emotionally by the other.

This position communicates the message that the other person is truly okay the way he/she is, which encourages self-acceptance. This, of course, is the most desirable basis for all self-growth and evaluation.

The **Fair Witness** is a position of choice. It is not the **best** position for all situations—it is simply a useful choice.

Conditions necessary for **Fair Witness Position:**

- Caring about person as a whole human being—not the problem or goal.
- Maintain boundaries—peripheral vision and hearing.
- Make eye contact
- Maintain energy as witness, present alert, attentive; non-evaluating, vulnerable to other
- No need to fix, help, change, judge

Note: There is a scene in *Stranger in a Strange Land,* by Robert Heinlein, where a visitor from another planet is looking at a field with cows in it. When asked to describe what he or she sees, the stranger replies, "Several animals with brown and white spots on the side of them closest to me."

Fair Witness Exercise
Based on the work of Anné Linden

1. Subject identifies a **Part** of him/her that seems to sabotage his/her Self-Esteem. A **Part** that you don't like—that you would rather not have.

2. Subject fully becomes this **Part**.

3. Guide steps into **Fair Witness Position** and maintains it for the rest of the interaction. Guide begins to dialogue with the **Part**.

Note: If subject begins to come out of being the **Part**, e.g., comments **about** the **Part**, guide gently and firmly assists subject in staying fully **in** the **Part**.

4. Guide must be present and actively involved with the **Part** while not allowing him/herself to get into fixing or helping. Maintain acceptance of what is. Ask questions like:

"How/what are you thinking/feeling?"

"What do you want?"
"What don't you want?"
"What is your name?"
"Who are you?"
"Tell me about yourself."
"What is important to you?"
"What makes you afraid?"
"What makes you sad?"
"And what's that like?"
"And where are you?"
"And what happens next?"
"And how old are you?"
"And is there anything else?"
"And how do you know that?"
"And how do you feel about that?"

(You can make up your own questions as long as they are this type and designed to encourage the person/**Part** to express him/herself—no judgmental or helping questions.)

The purpose of this dialogue is to give the person/**Part** the space, time, and opportunity to express self. To talk about his/her emotions, thoughts, desires, hatreds, etc. It is not the purpose to help, fix, change, comfort the person/**Part**. Maintain a dialogue in this manner for a full 8 minutes.

5. Thank the **Part** for speaking with you. Assist Subject in Reintegrating, i.e., bringing the **Part** back in self of the whole person.

6. Guide steps out of **Fair Witness Position**. Ask Subject what his/her experience is now of that **Part** and of the overall process.

Note: Switch roles and repeat process.

Internal Fair Witness
Based on the work of Anné Linden

It is useful and desirable to have an internal **Fair Witness Part**.

This process describes how to create one, or if person already has this part, to enhance, strengthen, and open channels of communication with this **Part**.

1. Ask Subject to go inside self and find his/her **Fair Witness Part**. "Go within self to your **Fair Witness** and connect with it in some way."

Note: If the person cannot locate this **Part**—even after asking his/her unconscious to help identify and connect with it, then ask the Subject to identify some person he/she knows who can be non-judgmental, accepting and involved (rather than aloof or detached). Have Subject make an image of this person, remember types of things he/she says, how he/she speaks, facial expressions, posture, etc. Subject then imagines creating own part based on this model. "What would it be like to have an internal part like this person?"

2. Subject:

   a. Locate where in the body this **Part** is: Back of head, right shoulder, mid-chest, left side, knee, etc.
   b. What does it look like: color, shape, size, focus (**Note**: the **Part** does **not** have to have a human form—it can be symbolic, animal, plant, etc.—even though it can talk).
   c. What does the **Part** say: words, phrases, messages? How does it sound: volume, tonal, tempo?
   d. What sensation is connected to this **Part**: pressure, expansion, vibration, warmth, coolness, etc.?
   e. Put all the above information together and practice experiencing/perceiving this **Part**.

3. Subject asks **Part** to give him/her a special signal that is unique to it: a special sound, flash of color, a certain sensation, or word. Subject will then know when he/she is in contact with this **Part**.

4. Subject thinks of some situation that troubles his/her Self-Esteem. Ask **Fair Witness Part** for its perspective regarding this

situation. Dialogue with **Part**. If necessary, Subject can become own **Fair Witness** and look at, listen to the situation in question.

Note: Remember always to have Subject return to whole self.

Thank **Fair Witness Part.**

5. Ask subject what he/she learned.

Index Computations
Based on the work of Richard Bandler and John Grinder

Index Computations are the distinctions within one's own self and another. It is often useful to notice which of the above possibilities a person pays more attention to in a given context or situation. It is important in self-awareness—distinguishing feeling, thinking and doing.

Experience can be divided into **Index Computations**:

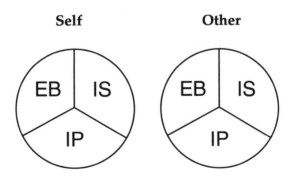

| **Self** | **Other** |

EB | IS

IP

EB | IS

IP

E B = External Behavior   talking, gestures, etc.   **Doing**

I S = Internal State   overall feeling state   **Feeling**

I P = Internal Processes   computations, thinking   **Thinking**

Modal Operators
Based on the work of Richard Bandler, John Grinder, Anné Linden

Modal Operators define words that operate on the mood of the main process word (verb) in a sentence. They qualify the experience. **For example**: *I want to exercise.* Exercise is the main verb; *want* is the modal operator. I *should* exercise. I *have to* exercise. I *can* exercise. I *will* exercise. I *need to* exercise. Each model operator changes the entire impact or mood of the sentence even though no other words are changed.

Properties of Modal Operators

1. Directionality: Toward or Away

> Determined by the presence or absence of the negative form of the modal operator.
> **Example**: want/don't want, can/can't, will/won't.

2. Involvement: Reactive or Proactive

> **Reactive**: Receptive—passive (The world does to me. The world acts on me. The world controls me.)
> **Proactive**: Active—Initiate (I do to the world—I act upon the world. I control the world.)

Reactive or **Proactive** is a digital distinction—that is, you are either one or the other at a particular moment in time. Within each distinction, Reactive or Proactive, there is a continuum from more to less. **For example**: the difference between **can** and **hope**, or **want** and **will**. Both can and hope are reactive; however, hope is more passive than can. Want and will are both proactive; however, **will** is more active than **want**.

Linguistically Modal Operators fall into three categories:

> **Necessity**: need to, have to, should, etc;
> **Possibility**: can, able to, etc;

Contingency: might, could, etc. These distinctions are not as relevant as **Directionality** and **Involvement** when identifying, adjusting and creating powerful self-talk Modal Operator sequences.

Directionality of Modal Operators (Toward/Away) is determined by the presence or absence of the negative form.

Involvement of Modal Operators (Reactive/Proactive) is inherent in the individual Modal Operator itself. This does not change with a change in direction or specific content.

Following are two lists of Modal Operators organized according to their involvement. (All are represented in their positive form.)

Reactive	Proactive
Should	Want
Can	Will
Ought to	Have to
Supposed to	Must
Need	Choose to
May	Dare
Might	Deserve to
Able	Got to
Possible	Determined to
Try	
Hope	
Wish	
Could	
Would	

Examples of Modal Operator Sequences:
(Self-Talk)

I want to • have to • will . . .
I want to • can't • have to • will . . .
I hope to • could • can . . .
I can should • have to • must . . .

I have to • won't • could • might . . .
I've got to • got to • have to • have to • won't • will • won't
• have to • must . . .
I've got to • don't got to • do I want to • have to • will . . .
I should • can't • can • want • need • have to • will . . .
I have to • I got to • won't • will . . .
I got to • don't got to • do I need? • will I? • will . . .

Non-Polar Thinking
Based on the work of Anné Linden

This type of thinking is the opposite of dichotomous, either/or,
right/wrong types of thinking. It is "options thinking." Rather
than experiencing a situation as black or white, one perceives
many gradations of grey. Non-polar thinking supports non-judgmental observation and acceptance of what is.

Basic to this type of thinking is the ability to observe and report
sensory-based experience. For example: In a difficult or
challenging experience rather than judge whether it is good or
bad, or that your behavior is positive or negative, you would
place your attention on what you see, hear and physically feel.
You report this information in sensory-based language. (See list
of sensory-based language, pgs. 192-198.) This tends to expand
your experience of the situation, increase your available
information, and support optional thinking.

Non-Polar Exercise

1. Pick one of the following topics with which you continue to
experience difficulties and limitations: authority, commitment,
intimacy, success, anger, control, vulnerability.

2. Within the frame of the topic, identify a situation in which
you experienced yourself as **Right** and a situation in which you
experienced yourself as **Wrong**.

3. Create a movie of the **Right** situation.

a. **See through your own eyes**. Concentrate on what you can see: colors, shapes, sizes, location of objects and people, quality of light and shadow, patterns, background, foreground, etc. Repeat this but **see yourself** in the situation and concentrate on what you see.

b. Re-run the movie. This time concentrate on what you can hear: volume, location of sounds, pitch, tempo, rhythm, silence, background and foreground, etc.

c. Re-run the movie. This time concentrate on what you feel physically—**not emotionally**. Movements, pressure, temperature, location in body, duration, moisture, tactile sensations, etc.

d. Re-run the movie **backward** from the end to the beginning: seeing self in movie.

e. Re-run the movie three times faster than normal; first from beginning to end, and then backwards from end to beginning.

4. Repeat Step 3 with the **wrong** situation.

5. Think of both these situations. Are you still right and wrong? What new information have you gotten? What are you aware of now? What is different? What have you learned?

Note: If you have any trouble seeing inner pictures or hearing inner words/sounds, simply ask yourself, "If I could see this image or hear this, what would it look/sound like?" Describe it to self and continue.

Perceptual Positions
Based on the work of Robert Dilts & Connie Rae Andreas

Perceptual Positions refer to three possible perspectives a person can assume during an interaction with another.

First Position: Self—Associated—inside self. Seeing, hearing and feeling from within one's own self.

Second Position: Observer—Dissociated—Meta Position. This is an observer position—you are seeing and hearing yourself and have feelings **about** the situation rather than of the situation.

Third Position: Other—Associated to the other—becoming the other person so that you see through his/her eyes, hear through his/her ears and take on his/her feelings.

Summary: 1st Position: Self
              2nd Position: Observer
              3rd Position: Other

Well-Formedness Conditions For Aligned Perceptual Positions
Based on the work of Robert Dilts & Connie Rae Andreas

A Perceptual Position is Aligned when all major Representation Systems (Visual, Auditory, Kinesthetic) are aligned in each Position:

1. When in **1st Position,** your visual, auditory and kinesthetic system is originating/coming from within **self**. Use pronouns I/you, he/she.

2. When in **2nd Position,** your visual, auditory and kinesthetic system is originating/coming from your **observer** position— Meta Position. Use pronouns her/him, they/them.

Special conditions for 2nd Position:

  a. Your observer position must be at eye level with self and others in the experience. Be sure you are not looking at self and others from above or below eye level.
  b. Your observer position must be equidistant from self and the other. Be sure you are not closer to self or to other.

3. When in **3rd Position** your visual, auditory and kinesthetic

system is originating/coming from the other. Use pronouns I/ you, he/she.

Perceptual Positions Process
Based on the work of Robert Dilts and Connirae Andreas

1. Identify an interaction with someone else that is limiting.

2. Determine which positions the subject's feeling, visual and auditory are coming from.

Note: In any limiting interaction the person will not be aligned in one position. His/her visual, auditory, kinesthetic will be coming from different positions.

Ask, "What are you aware of?" "What do you see, hear, feel?"

Listen for where these systems are—what positions. Clue: use of pronouns:

#1—Self:	I—You—He/She
#2—Observer:	Her/Him—They/Them
#3—Other:	You—Me

3. a. Have person re-live the situation and be in **1st Position**. Assist him/her to align all systems in that position. Talk them through it—see through your eyes, hear what's going on around you, get in touch with **your** feelings. Essentially you are helping him/her to associate fully in all three systems.

   b. Have person re-live situation and be in **2nd Position**. Assist him/her to align all systems in the Observer Position. See self and other—Hear self and talk to yourself about what is going on (meta comment)—Have feelings **About** the situation in which you are one step removed. Make sure that person is seeing self and others at eye level and is equidistant from self and other.

    c. Have person re-live situation and be in **3rd Position**. Assist him/her to align all systems in that position. See through his/her eyes, hear through his/her ears, have his/her feelings. You're looking and listening to her/him (actually him/herself) as this other person. Become the other.

4. Take the person through all three positions several times.

    a. Re-experience the situation from beginning to end from each fully aligned,position.

    b. Have person re-experience the situation, and shift them rapidly from one position to another.

5. Have person think of what was this limiting situation. Check what is his/her limiting situation. Check what his/her experience is now—what new information have he/she gotten? What can he/she do in the future?

Phobia Trauma Process
Based on the work of Richard Bandler and John Grinder

The process, with 3-step dissociation and variations, can be used for any overwhelming negative response—a past experience that is intensely limiting and the person, when faced with a stimulus associated with the experience, has no choice but to re-live the emotions with the same or increased intensity of the original experience. This is often accompanied by strong physical reactions.

1. **Person thinks of the traumatic experience.**

    Programmer calibrates.

2. **Programmer establishes rapport**—and a strong feeling of security and safety with client (reassure client that you (programmer) will **not** let him/her fall back into those phobic feelings/experiences).

Establish a strong, positive anchor of present, here and now feelings of competence—abilities to take care of self; confidence in self. Elicit and anchor #1. Anchor in one spot, stacking if necessary to make very strong.

3. **Ask client to identify one of the first times** he/she remembers having this phobic (or phobic type) or traumatic response. Beware of your language—asking for the first experience may elicit an evaluation and inhibit the client's unconscious. **Instruct client to "freeze the first frame"** of the earlier experience. **Ask him/her to see younger self in detail** in this first frame—just **before** anything stressful or upsetting begins to happen.

It is crucial that the programmer keep calibrating client and **not** allow him/her to fall into and begin to re-experience the phobic/traumatic feelings. If this does begin to happen, bring client back to safety of here and now where he/she is competent, capable, adult, etc.

4. **Have client establish a point of view** that will allow him/her to see him/herself sitting with you (programmer) in the present time/space coordinates. Then have client see him/herself **watching a movie** of **younger self** in **that** experience that happened **then**. You can establish a movie screen/TV screen, etc. on which he/she can watch the movie of **that past experience.** This is a 3-step dissociation and it is useful since it serves as extra protection against person collapsing back into the phobic/traumatic experience.

Client's Perspective	Client Here and Now	The Younger Self in Phobic/ Traumatic Experience

Anchor this auditorily.

5. **Hold Anchor #1 and use voice and words to auditorily anchor 3-step dissociation. Instruct client to let the movie of the past experience run,** telling client that he or she will learn something

new and important from this experience. As client is watching self watch her younger self, the programmer should reinforce the dissociation verbally—"As you continue to watch yourself sitting **here** safe and comfortable next to me in my office on Tuesday, April, etc. watching a **younger** you go through **that** experience **then**."

If at any time client begins to fall into phobic/traumatic feelings, reinforce the dissociation and the resource anchor. If that does not work bring the client back to here and now—re-establish safety and confidence and begin again. You can use submodalities to reinforce dissociation: make the movie of past experience very small, far away, defocused, etc., until client can tolerate a more "normal" representation. Another variation is to have the client see self in the past movie.

6. **When client finishes watching the old experience, release anchor #1** and instruct client to float back into here-and-now body. From that perspective, have client look at younger self at end of that experience—comfort and reassure younger self that he/she made the best choice available; and at the time did the best that could be done and that the present self appreciates that what the other self is today partly results from what younger self went through then. Reassure younger self that he/she is going to be all right—that the here-and-now client knows that, since he/she is the younger self's future.

Instruct client to do whatever it takes to reassure and comfort and get younger self to believe that present self appreciates him/her. When younger self looks comforted and reassured, instruct present self to bring him/her back inside present self.

Reintegration

7. **Test**: Have client think of original phobia or trauma. Behavioral test if possible.

Note: If necessary, this can be done several times. If there's still some phobic or traumatic feelings present, this might be an indication that that reaction/feeling is serving some positive intention and a reframe would be necessary.

Fast Phobia Process
Based on the work of Richard Bandler

Note: This process is only appropriate with single phobias that do **not** involve the client's sense of identity.

Before doing Fast Phobia Process, check carefully whether the client is truly ready to give up the phobia and not have it in his/her life. Check the ecology of **not** having this phobia—that it does **not** benefit the client in any way that he/she is not willing to let go of.

1. **Identify phobia** or phobic-type response.

2. **Identify one of the earliest memories** of this phobia

3. **Make a black and white dissociated** (see younger self) movie of this experience and run it from beginning to end at four (4) times faster than normal speed.

4. **Freeze final frame**. Turn the light up until you get a white-out. Turn light back to normal. Step inside own image (Associate), bring back color and run movie backwards, at normal speed, to the beginning of memory.

5.**Do Steps 3 and 4 from 8-15 times**. Test. Think of phobia. Put self in situation that was phobic.

Note: Be sure your voice tempo is congruent with the instructions you are giving the client. Your tempo should not be **slow** when instructing the client to do something four times normal speed. Ask client to indicate with a nod of his/her head when reaching the end of the movie memory and when reaching the beginning. This will assist your tracking and calibration.

Reclaim Personal History
Based on the work of Anné Linden

This process is useful to strengthen a specific resource and positive sense of self.

1. **Identify Resource** you want to strengthen. Name it with a word or short phrase.

2. **Access experience of Resource,** associate and relive. **Anchor.** (R - Anchor) This can be a self-anchor or an auditory/kinesthetic combined or separate anchor.

3. **Hold R Anchor** and go back through time and space (past personal history) and identify 3-5 other examples of experience of Resource. These examples may be in very different contexts and scattered through time. Name each example with a few words.

4. **Return to present time**. Release R Anchor. Review briefly examples. Hold R Anchor and go back to each example, associate and re-live fully each experience. Do this with all examples, and continue to hold R Anchor.

5. **Return to present time**. Release R Anchor. Imagine time in future when Resource would be desirable. Hold anchor and live future situation. Do this several times with several different situations.

6. **Test**: Imagine future situations and do not fire Anchor.

Reframing
Based on the work of Richard Bandler and John Grinder

Reframing is the skill of changing perceptions about something that has been labeled a problem, bad or negative. Human beings put frames around experiences in order to organize them and give them meaning. For example we frame whole categories of experiences as good, bad, pleasurable, painful, appropriate, inappropriate, etc.

In reframing we change the frame, thereby changing the meaning and the category of the experience. This is built upon two assumptions:

1. There is a difference between behavior and intention: separation of behavior and intention.

$$\frac{\text{Behavior}}{\text{Intention}}$$

EXPERIENCE

2. There is a positive intention beneath every behavior: this intention (what we sometimes call meta outcome, purpose or function) concerns the life of the person doing the behavior. It is not directed outward toward others, but inward toward the person.

Positive intentions fall into two categories: **Protection** and **Motivation**.

For example:
   Behavior: an Internal Voice that tells person "You're stupid."
   Intention: to motivate person to try harder and accomplish more.

   Behavior: being late
   Intention: to nurture person by having them take time for
                 themselves.

One Word Reframes:
Thrifty .... Stingy
Responsible............................. Boring
Spontaneous .... Unpredictable
Funny .... Childish

Concerned .... Overbearing
Confidence .... Arrogance

Parts

"Parts of the psyche detach themselves from consciousness and lead an autonomous life of their own."—Carl Jung

"A part is not just a temporary emotional state or habitual thought patterns. Instead it is a discreet and autonomous mental system that has an idiosyncratic range of emotion, style of expression and set of abilities, intentions or functions."—Richard Schwartz

Parts are metaphors for different aspects and qualities of a person. Each person is a whole, individual entity with an essential core. However, each person has many different aspects to his/her personality—he/she is actually a community or family of **parts**. The longer we live and accumulate experience and knowledge, the more **parts** we develop. **Parts** are derived from the **roles** we play in life: mother, brother, friend, teacher, boss, peacemaker, problem-solver, healer, writer, etc.; and our **attributes**: compassionate, angry, assertive, gentle, fearful, vulnerable, perfectionist, vengeful, envious, impatient, etc.

Make a list of the various roles you fill in your life, and another of your attributes (these are often experienced as emotions). From these identify what you think are your most significant **Parts**. These can include ones you appreciate and like and also those you want to get rid of. You can name these **parts** as seems appropriate: Little Girl, Tarzan, Wimp, Manager, Easy-Going, Ambitious, Hector, etc.

When working with **Parts**, note an essential and underlying presupposition: a **Part** is made up of the **behavior** it generates and the **intention** or function it serves within the overall person's community of **Parts**. This intention or function is always positive within this inner system.

Note: This concept is important for the **6-Step** and **Spacial Reframe**.

6-Step Reframe
Based on the work of Richard Bandler and John Grinder

Presupposition: There is a distinction between intention and behavior, and the intention is positive within the person's own psyche.

The main purpose of reframing, besides creating more positive options for a limiting behavior, is to establish bridges (channels of communication) between client's unconscious and conscious minds and between parts of the unconscious—to enable the client to discover that all parts are allies, potential teachers and friends.

1. **Identify behavior client wants more choices about.**

2. **Have client ask part responsible for Behavior X** if it's willing to communicate with client's conscious mind, then just to wait for a signal—possibly in words, but more likely to be expressed as some change in images, sounds, sensations. **Yes/No signal**: To check answer: if answer **yes**, Ask part to **increase** that image, sound, sensation, if answer is **no, decrease**. **If answer is yes**, thank **part** and go on. **If answer is no**, thank **part** for communicating and reassure part that it is entirely understandable that it does not trust client's conscious mind and it can continue to communicate on an unconscious level. Reassure part that it is in charge of behavior X and in no way are you (programmer) trying to get rid of it nor would you allow the client to attempt to do so. We are only trying to get some information.

3. **Ask part what purpose or function it has**—what is its positive intention? **Part** can answer consciously or unconsciously (see Step 4, note). You must get the client to accept that there is a positive intention and to begin to appreciate that **part** as a friend/ally and teacher. Thank **part** for positive intention and make sure

client begins to sincerely appreciate **part**. If **part** at first answers in negative, keep asking the question—and trust that if you peel the onion far enough, you will find the positive core.

4. **Ask client to go to creative part** (creative unconscious) and ask it to generate at least 3 alternatives to behavior X that would satisfy intention—i.e., accomplish the purpose of behavior X. **Note**: You can have **part** responsible for **behavior** X go to the **creative part** directly to inform that **part** what its positive intention is. This is useful especially when positive intention remains unconscious. These new choices can be conscious or on unconscious level; ask **creative part** to give the client a signal when it has generated at least three new alternatives. Thank **creative part**.

5. **Ask part responsible for behavior X** to review the alternatives and to pick the one(s) best able to fulfill that **part's** intention. Ask **part** if it will use alternative(s) instead of **Behavior** X. **Do yes/no signal** (see Step 2). **If yes**, thank part and go on. **If no**, put a time limit on request, e.g., two weeks, etc. to try out alternative(s) to find out which is **most** effective. **If still no**, ask part to go back to **creative part** and help generate alternatives it would be willing to try out at least for a limited time. Thank **part**.

6. **Ecological Check: Ask the client to check with all parts** to make sure they accept the agreement worked out between client and part responsible. **If yes**, thank all parts. **If no**, check how the client knows this. Then ask that the image, sound, word sensation **increase** if indeed this represents an objection, decrease/disappear if it's not an objection (apparent objections sometimes turn out to be signals of excitement, enthusiasm, etc.)

Reassure the client that any objection is important information and is welcome. Objections tell you what you need. If there is an objection, go back to Step 3 and go through process with **part** that objects, making sure that the **objecting part** and the **part responsible** for Behavior X agree on the alternative behaviors and can work together. Treat **parts** of the client as though they were **all parts** of a negotiating team. It is important that each member's function and purpose be respected and paid attention to. Cycle back through process until you get full acceptance for any alternative behaviors from all **parts** involved. Thank all **parts**.

Sometimes during a **6-Step Reframe** an objection surfaces that represents a **part** that is in serious conflict with **part** responsible for the original limiting behavior. In that case, a **Spacial Reframe** is necessary.

Note: **6-Step Reframe** is useful to do in order to gather information about a client's internal parts. Sometimes it is necessary to do this process several times around the same issue: the client often needs to be trained in doing this process. Each time through the process serves to better install a very useful strategy for dealing with limitations and change.

6-Step Reframes are usually done with **behaviors** (internal or external) or **symptoms**; e.g., nail biting, blushing, being late, internal negative messages or images, headaches, pain, fatigue, etc.

Spacial Reframe™
Taken from the work of Anné Linden

The process is for use with problems resulting from inner conflict. The purpose is to separate two parts that are in conflict and establish a common outcome and a means of communication between them, so that they can begin to work together and with the whole person.

1. **Identify and clearly separate the parts**. Establish a chair for each part. Instruct the client that upon sitting in either chair, he/she will become that part as fully as possible. Explain that you will be speaking directly to each part. Ask client to name each part to further facilitate separation and tracking.

2. **Begin your communication with part** #1 by asking for its meta-outcome, what it wants for the whole person. Get specific

information: What is part's purpose/function/intention? Have client disengage him/herself from part #1 and move to the space of part #2. Repeat the information-gathering process with part #2.

Establish some commonality of purpose/function/intention for parts. You can go back and forth between the parts, eliciting from each the outcome of the outcome, until you clarify what each part ultimately wants for the whole person. Chunk up.

You need to establish some outcome for the whole person that both parts can agree to—keep eliciting the outcome of the outcome until you get agreement. Chunk up—to a more general outcome that both can agree to.

3. **Negotiate with each part on what each wants for** itself and **from** the other part. Find out how each part would know if it was getting from the other what it wants. Find out what each part is willing to do for/give to the other part.

Use your calibration skills and flexibility to get each part to recognize the other and to appreciate some attribute of the other—so that each part is willing to learn from and respect the other. Either part must recognize **some** value in the other—no matter how small. Sometimes it is useful to ask one part to imagine what it would be like if the other part were **totally** gone.

At this point it may be appropriate to set up signals between the parts so that each can be aware when the other needs something—time, space, permission, appreciation, attention, affection, etc. Get each part congruently to agree to at least **some** of what the other wants from it.

It is often enough to simply get the parts to agree to begin the process of recognition and friendship. Sometimes it is too big a chunk to expect parts that may have been warring with each other for years to totally accept and love each other in an hour's time.

4. Once some level of agreement is reached, and ways established for each **part** to be taken care of (i.e., alternatives to the way they have been fighting and conflicting that are acceptable to both), have the client sit in another place—it could be the chair he/she started out in—and see both parts. Have the client find out if the parts look, feel, sound satisfied with the negotiated alternatives—or at least with the process of getting to know each other in a new and different way.

Do not integrate the conflicting parts unless that is totally acceptable to both, and this is rare. It is enough, and often more ecological, for the parts to retain their separate identities and simply acknowledge each other's values (and perhaps join hands).

At this point, have the client bring both (or all) of the parts back inside him/herself.

Test: Put person in context of conflict, either an actual situation or else a fantasy one. Calibrate. If not satisfactory, go back and find out where and what the objection is, and negotiate some acceptable alternatives.

Spacial Reframe Procedure Questions ᔆᴹ
Taken from the work of Anné Linden

Presupposition: Both parts have positive intentions toward whole person and are beneficial in some way.

Purpose: To create a way for parts to communicate to get to know and acknowledge each other, to learn to work together while recognizing and appreciating each other's differences and values.

Note: A useful way to sequence the following questions is: Do Steps 1 and 2 with each part; then do Steps 3, 4, 5, with each part; then do Steps 6 and 7 with each part.

Ask Each Part:

1. What do you want for whole person?

2. What will that do for him/her?

    Chunk up until you get agreement that both want the same thing.

3. What do you want for self?

    (What will that do for you?)—use this question here only if necessary.

4. What do you want from other part?

    (What will that do for you?)—use this question here only if necessary.

5. How will you know you're getting what you want from other part? (What will you see, hear, sense?)

6. What can you learn from/benefit from other part? How is the other part of value to you?

7. What are you willing to do for or give the other part? (What can each part learn from the other part. Of what value is each part to the other?)

Work out specifics; create signals if necessary—when, where, what, how much/how often, etc.

Parts Play
Based on the work of Anné Linden

4 People CC - Subject; DD, EE, FF - Players

1. CC identifies a desired goal/change that he/she is not achiev-

ing and an objection to this change/goal. CC assigns to DD, EE or FF the parts of her responsible for (1) the outcome; (2) the objection, and then picks the person who will be the negotiator. A teaches the players how to play the parts of him/her who represent the goal and objection: the words to say, tonality, tempo, facial expressions, posture, etc.

2. CC describes the context/environment in which he/she wants this goal. The parts must act out their scenarios within this context.

3. The negotiator's task is to get agreement between the parts that it is okay to have the goal within this context.

Agreement Procedure

    a. What is each part's positive function/intention—the positive meta outcome?
    b. What does each part want for him/herself and from the other part?
    c. How can these parts congruently agree to the desired goal, to work out an acceptable compromise/agreement. Negotiate or work out some agreement, even if it is only to continue to talk to each other about their disagreement. Important to find down to **something** they can agree to— no matter how small.
    d. Once parts have agreed to something, they can join hands
      . . . .

4. CC observes this entire process. Only if person playing one of his/her parts seriously misrepresents the part can CC interrupt and correct the role play. At the point where parts join hands, CC takes their hands, moving together in a close circle until the three pairs of hands touch and become as one.

5. Negotiate the future—pace to a future time when this agreement can be called upon. CC then symbolically takes his/her goal part and objection back inside—Reintegration.

Representational Systems
Derived from the work of Richard Bandler and John Grinder

Representational Systems are the sensory systems (see, hear, feel, smell and taste) that we use to represent (think about) our experiences. When we remember, make decisions, motivate ourselves or do any other mental activity, we represent our thought primarily in images, sounds and/or words, and feelings. These we call our representational systems. To identify which representational system a person is using, pay attention to the type of language and/or eye movement patterns. We have included a sample list of words (Predicates) and an eye movement chart (Funny Face) to help you understand and use Representational Systems.

Predicates

Predicates are process words (verb, adverbs, adjectives) that describe a dynamic process rather than something static. Predicates indicate what sensory system the person is most conscious of: Visual, Auditory, Kinesthetic, Olfactory, Gustatory. Kinesthetic is divided into two categories: **Primary**: that which we experience directly, as in movements, visceral, tactile, proprioceptive, temperature, pressure; and **Meta/Emotional**, which refers to emotions that result from sensory experience, either internal or external. Predicates indicate what a person is aware of: eye movements and other accessing cues indicate processing information that a person **may** be conscious of **or** information that is out of conscious awareness.

Visual Sensory System

visualize	glow	eclipse	disillusion
watch	radiate	overshadow	illuminate
reflect	oversight	espy	peer
blank	overview	scan	clear
enlighten	foggy	elucidate	see

shine
look
view
show
mirror
reveal
illusion
(to) eye
photograph
foresight
angle
horizon
insight

focus
gaze
frame
stare
luminous
peruse
colorful
blue
perspective
outlook
color
illustrate

glance
hazy
darken/lighten
vague
crystal clear
twinkle
veil
reflect
scene
image
blur
notice

apparition
obscure
appear
flash
imagine
shed light
vision
picture
paint
hindsight
bright
outlook

Auditory Sensory System

rhythm
rhyme
beat
row
snap
swear
echo
remark
state
tune
unhearing
buzz
divulge
pronounce
voice
argue
hush
cry
speechless
invocate
announce
moan

click
say
expand
noise
chime in
attune
overtone
question
unhearing
sound
whistle
exclaimed
roar
rumor
utter
taciturn
propose
squeak
groan
rebuff
articulate
harmony

discordant
whining
chiming
spell out
raspy
pitch
wail
hear
listen
sound
make music
silence
resonate
screech
talk
mention
imagine
oral
growl
retort
audible

deaf
mellifluous
dissonance
din
cacophony
quiet
silent
hum
purr
be heard
mute
wail
shrill
squeal
tell
gossip
loud
proclaim
whistle
cackle
boisterous

Primary Kinesthetic Sensory System (directly experienced)

motion	bounce	scratch	
blistering	touch	throbbing	pull
sway	grope	chew	cast
pressure	hold	feverish	break
slip	roll	warm	catch
crush	sweat	vibrate	tap
cast	hike	rough/smooth	grasp
seize	grind	throw	shape
stuck	numb	turn	squishy
sticky	move	drive	movement
tied	hang	swallow	hit
feel	backbone	loose	rigid
stirring	scrape	support	tight
drive	run	balance	equilibrium
walk	firm	penetrate	grab
kick	block	hot	soft
cold	luke warm	sore	sharp
hard			

Meta Kinesthetic Sensory System (emotional)

tranquil	emotional	agitate	frustrated
emote	pressured	nervous	blissful
passionate	energetic	weary	penitent
affectionate	tired	joyful	lonely
calm down	stuck	exasperated	complacent
relaxed	embarrassed	delighted	(dis)enchant
relieve	feel	crushed	morose
annoy	bored	warm (emotion)	stressful
upset	unfeeling	perturbed	depression
disgusted	happy	panic	anxious
fed up	sad	joyful	grateful
glum	glad	inspired	peaceful
horrified	mad/angry	suffer	terrorized
exuberant	aroused	ecstatic	

Olfactory Sensory System

stink	smell	flowery	putrid
sniff	odor	aroma	rancid
stale	fragrant	acrid	rotten
perfumed	smoky	pungent	musty
fresh			

Gustatory Sensory System
(some are also **Primary Kinesthetic**)

eat it up	nibble	licks	fishy
mouth-watering	munch	sweet	flavorful
palatable	bite	sour	fruitful
lick	devour	peppery	meaty
swallow	smacks	bitter	lean
digest	crumby	bland	drink in
chomp	tasteless(ful)	insipid	spicy
oily	savor	half baked	regurgitate

Unspecified

sense	recognize	demonstrate	connect
experience	realize	ambiguous	generate
understand	read	cancel	disturb
think	attend to	emphasize	relate
learn	comprehend	blend	support
process	appreciate	guess	challenge
decide	discern	calibrate	wonder
motivate	ponder	associate	aware of
consider	remember	believe	interrupt
change	create	deceive	suppose
perceive	examine	integrate	pretend
(in)sensitive	sensation	proceed	intuit
conceive	memorize	cerebrate	know
conscious	(in)congruent	concentrate	compute

PREDICATE PHRASES

Visual	Auditory	Kinesthetic
beyond a shadow of doubt	rings a bell	be on your toes
bird's eye view	give me your ear	come to grips with
eye to eye	tattle-tale	get a handle on
get the picture on	tell the truth	hang in there
look the other way	tuned in/out	keep your shirt on
sight for sore eyes	hidden message	set your cards on the table
mind's eye	word for word	stuffed shirt
flashed on	talk me through	stiff upper lip
		sharp as a tack

PREDICATES TRANSLATED ACROSS SYSTEMS

Unspecified	Visual	Auditory	Kinesthetic
attitude	perspective/viewpoint	comment/opinion	stance/position
consider	look over	sound out	feel out
persevere	see through	hear out	carry through/ stick with it
demonstrate	show/illustrate	explain	walk through
emit	radiate/sparkle	resonate	vibrate/pulsate
absent	blank	dumbfounded/silence	numb
plain	lackluster	muted	dull
ostentatious	flashy/colorful/showy	loud/screaming	slick/striking
attentive	look after	listen in on	care for
ignore	overlook	tune out	pass over/let slide
display	show off	sound off	put on parade
notice	look around	listen in	feel out
understand	get the picture	clicks into/tune in	catch on/grasp/ get the drift
identify	point out	call attention to	point out/put finger on
conceive	imagine	call up (recall)	get a hold of
recognize	eyeful	earful	stomach/handful
remind one of	look familiar	ring a bell	strikes one
rehearse	review	repeat	rerun
demonstrate	illuminate	instruct	lead through

refer to	point to	allude to	touch upon
attend to	look at	tune into	get a feel for
insensitive	blind	deaf	unfeeling
imitate	reflect/mirror	echo	bounce
balance	symmetry	harmony	tranquility
perceive	see	hear	feel
intensity	brightness	volume	pressure
pompous	gaudy	bombastic	pushy
overwhelming	eyeful	earful	stomach/handful
explore	look around	listen in	feel out
motivate	flash in	tune up	move/get into gear
remember	reflect	recall	re-feel
think	see	hear	feel
decide	see options	hear options	weigh options
	blind	deaf	numb
	disappear	fade out	melt

PREDICATES TRANSLATED ACROSS SYSTEMS

Visual	Auditory	Kinesthetic
gaudy	bombastic	pushy
sight	earshot	reach
eyeful	earful	stomach full (handful)
mess up	blow (something)	slip up
look around	listen in	feel out
disappear	fade out	melt (ease out)
look over	talk over	walk through
point out	call attention to	point out/finger
illustrate	talk/(someone) through	move (someone) through
	explain	direct
imagine	call up (recall)	get a hold of
look familiar	ring a bell	strikes one
review	rehearse	rerun
illuminate	open one's ears	uncover
illuminating	instructional	demonstrative
point to	allude to	touch upon
make someone see	convince	hammer home
flash on	tune into	get ahold of

come to see/get the picture		catch on, grasp get the drift
state of the art	last word	top drawer/ outstanding
bring light to	propose	put up to
blind	deaf	unfeeling
reflect	echo	bounce
mandala	mantra	asana
symmetry	harmony	tranquility/balance

Funny Face
Based on the work of Richard Bandler and John Grinder

Visual Constructed Vᶜ

Visual Remembered Vʳ

Auditory Constructed Aᶜ

Auditory Remembered Aʳ

Kinesthetic K

Auditory Digital Ad

PUPILS DILATED IS **VISUALIZATION**

Vᶜ—**Visual Constructed**—images/pictures never seen before, combinations never seen before (e.g. like seeing yourself in an experience) or seeing familiar images in new circumstances (e.g. floating in space).

Vʳ—**Visual Remembered**—images seen before—eidetic images—images from the past.

Aᶜ—**Auditory Constructed**—sounds or words which are being made up at the moment—new constructions (e.g. composing a speech).

A^r—**Auditory remembered**—sounds or words which are familiar (figures of speech, or cliches, or remembered tape loops), familiar tonalities, or tempos, songs.

K—**Kinesthetic**—(both meta/emotions and primary) feelings, emotions, body sensations, movements, proprioceptive feelings (like balance) and visceral sensations.

Ad—**Auditory Digital**—words, phrases, and sentences— internal dialogue—talk to yourself.

Smart Outcome Model
Derived from the work of Richard Bandler and John Grinder

A **Goal** and an **Outcome** are different distinctions. **Goals** can be general, non-specific, ill-formed desires or wishes. They can be very useful in motivation and in directing one's attention. However, **Outcomes** are specific and achievable. They form the basis of a map for guiding us toward the achievement of the outcome. There are rules for establishing a **Smart** (achievable) **Outcome**.

Structure of a Smart Outcome

All smart outcomes must conform to well-formedness conditions. Use these as a primary filter as you listen to people's goals or problems. When an outcome is well-formed it becomes realistic and achievable.

Well-Formedness Conditions for Outcomes

1. Stated in positives
2. Within individual's control
3. Sensory based description (testable)
4. Appropriately contextualized
5 Ecological

Outcome Frame

(Use meta-model to get clearly defined and specific information.)
1. What do you want?

Optional Step—Outcome Sequitor: What will having this outcome do for you? (Use this question to get the outcome to conform to the well-formedness conditions or to get something meaningful—something the person **really** wants)

2. **Evidence**: How will you know when you have achieved your outcome? What will you see, hear, feel?

3. **Context**: When, where, with whom do you want your outcome?

4. **Ecology**: How will this affect your life? Does not having this outcome benefit you in any way? What are the advantages and disadvantages of achieving this outcome?

Obstacles/Problem Frame

1. What stops you? (from getting your outcome)

2. How do you do this?

> Internal State (emotions)
> Internal Process (images, sounds, words, sensations)
> External Behavior (what do you do)

3. Trigger: What initiates the obstacle/problem state? What do you see/hear/do that triggers this?

4. Ecology: How does this obstacle/problem benefit you?

Note: Identify the most significant pieces of internal and/or external behavior that stops person from achieving outcome. If more than one piece, then identify the sequence in which these behaviors predictably occur.

Resources Frame

1. What resources do you already have that will assist you in achieving your outcome?

2. What resources or skills do you need in order to achieve your outcome?

Plan

1. Create a step-by-step plan for reaching your outcome:
   a. Change elements of the problem state
   b. Bring identified resources to bear on the outcome
   c. Go external and learn or acquire the skills/resources needed.

2. What is the first step you will take to achieve this goal? When?

Submodalities
Derived from the work of Richard Bandler

The best way to develop a **Representational System** is to explore **submodalities**: Become aware of them, practice changing and adjusting them—play with them. This will develop the system, giving you more awareness and choice. Of course, if there is an objection to developing a system, you must first take care of the objection. You can use **Reframing, Change History**, or **Reimprinting**. Before doing any submodality change work, **always** check the **ecology**; i.e., the effect on the entire fabric of the person's reality—physical, mental, emotional, spiritual, family, professional and social.

For example: a 30-year-old man came into therapy to develop self-esteem; it soon became apparent that he could not access his visual system. He could not bring his images into conscious awareness, much less identify the submodalities and adjust them. It turned out that when he was five years old, his younger sister and his mother were in a serious automobile accident in which his mother was killed. He **saw** this! His unconscious, in order to protect his ability to survive and go on with his life, blocked all images. At the time, the primary images were of his mother dying; if this survival mechanism had not clicked into place, he would have continually reaccessed those images and re-lived the trauma. This would have severely hampered his healing. However, at thirty he could handle those images, and what had been a healing decision at the time of the accident now became a serious limitation to his growth and evolution. A reframing intervention was done and this helped pave the way for him to begin to learn about his inner visual system, bring his pictures to unconscious and begin to play with the submodalities. This ability facilitated a better relationship with himself **and** with access to his images, he was better able to plan and create the type of future he wanted—to achieve his goals. This, of course, was good for his self-esteem.

Submodality Distinctions

Visual

Self in or out of the picture
Framed or panoramic
Color/black & white
Shade/hue—primary, pastels, muted, etc.
Brightness
Size of picture; distance of picture from self
Size of central object(s) (proportion)
Dimensionality (2D or 3D)
Intensity of color (or black & white); contrast
Movement (if so fast or slow); movie, still or slides

Focus (sharp or fuzzy); Focus (total or partial)
Angle viewed from (above, below, side)
Number of pictures (simultaneous/sequenced)
Tilt of picture (top, bottom, side, closer)
Location, contrast, shape
Foreground/background tunnel vision
Light source: transparent/opaque
Digital (words) or pictorial

Auditory

Volume
Cadence
  (interruptions, groupings)
Rhythm (regular, irregular)
Inflections (words marked
  out, how)
Tempo
Pauses
Pitch
Timbre (quality—where
  resonating from)

Uniqueness of sound
  (gravely, smooth, etc.)
Location
Monaural, stereo
Duration
Distance (from self)
Clarity
Contrast
Digital/tonal
Associated/dissociated
Background/foreground
Internal/external source

Kinesthetic /Primary

(**tactile**: skin senses;
  movement; pro-
  prioceptive: relational
  & balance; **visceral**:
  sensations usually
  represented in abdomen,
  chest or along midline
  of torso)
Temperature
Texture
Vibration

Pressure
Movement
Speed of movement
Duration (steady,
  intermittent)
Intensity Moisture
Location
Sequence
Frequency
Tingling
Hot—cold
Muscle tension
Sharp—dull
Duration
Intermittent (e.g.
  throbbing, etc.)

Kinesthetic/Emotional
Feelings about other perceptions or representations

Angry	Irritated	Excited	Sad
Afraid	Calm	Joyful	Loving, Etc.

Olfactory/Gustatory

Sweet	Salty
Sour	Burnt
Bitter	Aromatic

Submodalities
Derived from the work of Richard Bandler

Driving Submodality: The one submodality in an experience that drives the entire experience. When that submodality is changed it causes several other submodalities to change automatically—"the domino effect." And that submodality has a profound impact on the overall meaning and emotional tone of the experience.

Contrast Analysis: Taking two experiences (one desirable; the other limiting) in same or similar context, and eliciting their submodalities and contrasting the differences.

For Example: (in same context)

	CALM	AGITATED
VISUAL		
AUDITORY		
KINESTHETIC		

Mapping Across: After doing a Contrast Analysis transferring the submodalities of the desired experience to the limiting experience—changing the submodalities of the limiting experience to match those of the desired experience.

For example: If the images in the desired experience are panoramic and clearly focused and in the limiting experience they are framed and hazy, you make the image in the limiting experience panoramic and clearly focused.

Submodality Tasks
Based on the work of Richard Bandler

Work with Visual, Auditory and Kinesthetic distinctions. All these need to be done 5 or 6 times to make change permanent.

Note: After any change in submodality, go back to the original representation **before** doing another change.

1. Pick a pleasant experience and **change one submodality** at a time to discover which one makes the experience **more pleasant** and which one makes the experience **less pleasant**. (Example: move picture/voice closer, then further away. Or make picture/voice more focused, then less focused. Change size of picture, volume of voice).

2. Pick a slightly unpleasant experience: **change submodality** changes that made pleasant experience more pleasant to discover how to make unpleasant experiences less unpleasant or different.

3. Pick a pleasant experience: **add submodalities** one at a time to discover impact on experience. Do same with (mildly) unpleasant experience.

4. Pick a pleasant experience and **subtract submodalities** one at a time to discover impact on experience. Do the same with a mildly unpleasant experience.

5. Pick an unpleasant experience: run a movie of it, **play loud, happy music behind it.**

6. Pick an unpleasant experience and **put it into a kaleidoscope** and turn or fragment it.

7. Pick a mildly unpleasant memory: **run a movie** of the experience.

    a. Run it again and make yourself in color and the background in black and white.
    b. Run it again and make yourself move at double speed and context (background) at one half speed.
    c. Run it again and make yourself run at half speed.
    d. Run movie of the experience as you usually do—what is the impact on your feelings?

8. Pick a mildly unpleasant memory: **run a movie** of this experience.

    a. Run movie again and see yourself in it.
    b. Run movie again three times as fast.
    c. Run it again backwards at normal speed.
    d. Run it again forwards three times as slow.
    e. Run it again backwards three times as slow.
    f. Run it as you normally do—what is the impact on your feelings?

9. Pick a mildly unpleasant memory **run a movie** of this experience.

    a. Run again and see self.
    b. Run again and change angle/point-of-view—above, below, behind, etc.
    c. Run again and see/hear from out in space.
    d. Run again and tilt your lens (how you're seeing)
    e. Run again and spin your lens.

f. Run again the way you normally do. What is the impact on your feelings?

10. Pick a mildly unpleasant memory: **run a movie** of this experience. Determine **what sensory system (visual, auditory, kinesthetic)** you are **least aware** of.

a. Run movie again emphasizing this system, adding in as many of the submodalities of this system as possible. Do this three times.
b. Run the movie as you normally do. What is the impact on your feelings?

Changing Submodalities
Based on the work of Richard Bandler

1. **Change one submodality at a time**. Test how this changes the impact of experience. Does it **increase/decrease it positively or negatively**? (Do this several times to install a permanent change.) For example, make a picture more or less focused, bigger or smaller, make sound faster or slower, make texture rougher or smother, etc.

a. Do other submodalities change with the one deliberate change you made?
b. Can you change one submodality without the others changing? What makes this possible?
c. Are these changes one-way: if you change X, Y changes, but if you change Y, X doesn't change.
d. Are there changes in which the submodality changes only in one direction? You can increase (or decrease) X without a limit, but you can't decrease (or increase Y) beyond a certain point.
e. Which distinctions are analog (ones that vary continuously from zero to infinity in size or brightness), and which are digital distinctions (ones that are categorical/either-or; associated or dissociated).

2. **Adding submodality distinctions**: color, movement, texture, temperature, volume, etc. **Subtracting submodality distinctions**: delete color, movement, volume, etc. What are the effects of adding submodality distinctions as opposed to subtracting them? (Adding movement vs. subtracting movement.)

3. **Change viewpoint**: change point or angle of view: from above to below, from one side or another, from another's point of view (perceptual position change), see image, upside down, backward, inside out, etc.

4. **Fragmentation**: break picture into many, many fragments (e.g., broken windshield in car) for kaleidoscopic effect.

5. **Changing association**: separate self from context—see self in color and background(context) in black and white, move self at double speed and background (context), at half speed (vice versa), move self forward and background backward or vice versa.

Time Lines
Based on the work of Tad James, Wyatt Woodsmall, Anné Linden, Steve and Connirae Andreas

Time Lines affect our motivation, sense of self, access to resources and possibilities, and our ability to plan organize and shape our future. A well-formed Time Line (pp. 149-150) helps give one an overall sense of perspective about one's entire life and helps in maintaining emotional balance.

A Time Line is the spacial description of how a person organizes and understands his/her personal relationship to Time—his/her past, present and future. Until elicited, this organization remains unconscious.

Since time literally slips through our fingers—it is not something we can see, hear, touch, taste or smell—the only way we can compute time is in relationship to space. For example, "The future is before you," "Put that behind you," "Look ahead," "Leave that behind," "Grab the moment now."

It would seem that generally the future is in front of us and the past behind us. This is true only for some people; Time Lines are very idiosyncratic.

A person's Time Line is analogous to a path—the road traveled upon throughout life. The beginning is birth and the end is death—or perhaps not! We tend to relate to time/space from the perspective that has each one of us as a center that is surrounded by 3-dimensional space—360^0 in every direction. Upon this infinite grid of space, we superimpose a spatial organization reflecting our personal sense of time.

Identification of Time Lines
Based on the work of Tad James, Wyatt Woodsmall, Steve and Connirae Andreas, Anné Linden

1. Watch a person's gestures: he/she will literally "show" you where his/her past and future are.

2. Ask a person: "Where is your past—near and far, future—near and far, and present?" Get person to point to these and you will begin to get an outline of his/her Time Line. However, this is abstract and very personal and therefore can remain rather intellectual and perhaps be misleading.

3. This is a more specific and concrete method for identifying Time Lines:

   a. Ask person to identify something mundane that he/she does regularly. For example, taking a shower or brushing teeth or having a morning cup of coffee or eating dinner. It **must** be **mundane** and **regular**—no matter where the person is or what the circumstances are.

b. Ask the person to make a picture of doing this at various increments of time. For example, a month, six months, one year, two years, five years ago; in the past; now, a month from now, six month, one year, two years, five years from now and on into the future. You are asking the person to picture doing this mundane and regular activity at specific moments in the past, now and in the future.

c. Direct the person to indicate where each image is located in space. (If the person wants to put them all in same place, ask him/her to represent all the pictures of the various times simultaneously.)

d. Then simply draw a line between the indicated areas in space. This is much like "connecting the dots." You now have the beginning of the person's Time Line. It will have a particular shape. Sometimes, it is useful to label the shape.

You can now extend the line into the past right back to birth and into the future and the way to death.

Note: The present (now) is either represented immediately in front of the person or inside the person.

Well-Formedness Conditions For Time Lines
Based on the work of Anné Linden

Well-formedness conditions for Time Lines include:

1. The past is congruent with person's eidetic side and the future is congruent with their constructed side. For example, if the person is typically organized (eidetic images and tapes/sounds are on left) then the past should be represented somewhere to the left of the person and the future somewhere to the right. If the person is reversed, then the Time Line should be reversed.

2. The future is visible from the person's point of view—i.e., it is not blocked by the past or the present.

3. The past and future must be distinct and different from each other. That is, must be represented by different and distinct submodalities: location, size, color, light, distance, dimensionality. Besides location (spatial representation), there should be at least three other specific submodality distinctions between the past and future.

4. The Time Line must be continuous, with no breaks or gaps, and should go from birth to an ecological ending point.

Note: These are well-formedness conditions, meaning that these are the desirable parameters for a person's Time Line in order to facilitate the most ecological and successful relationship to time. Often a person's Time Line does not conform to these conditions and needs to be adjusted or changed.

Changing Time Lines
Based on the work of Tad James, Wyatt Woodsmall, Steve and Connirae Andreas, Anné Linden

It is essential that therapist adheres strictly to the well-formedness conditions when changing Time Lines.

When changing or working with Time Lines, it is useful to have person "float above his/her Time Line." Once the Time Line is established, have the person imagine he/she can literally "float" out of present body location and rise above self and self's Time Line. This is an interesting and informative position. Looking down on the Time Line from this position, the person can "see" his/her entire/whole Time Line and its overall shape. This process of "floating above the Time Line" is an important part of Time Line work.

1. Changing the desired submodalities one by one and then **rehearsing** this change until it "sticks"—allows the change to become automatic.

2. Changing the shape and/or location is actually only changing

a submodality and can be done all at once (e.g., reversing an entire Time Line) and then **"clicking"** into place. This usually "sticks" after only one try. The therapist can also change a section of the Time Line bit by bit until the person finds where it looks and feels best—then "click" it into place.

Notes: Whenever changing the location and/or shape, always "click" in into place. This helps to install the change. Calibrate and be sensitive to any change in a Time Line. As always, objections are information and must be respected and dealt with before proceeding with the change.

It is often useful and interesting to try on other people's Time Lines to experience the difference and get ideas.

Building A Future Time Line
Based on the work of Anné Linden

Sometimes a person does not have the future represented—no future Time Line, or the future extends only 3 to 5 years. (When a person has made an unconscious decision not to live longer than a parent, his/her Time Line will stop at that age.)

The following steps will help person build/create a future line:

Note: Be aware of objections to having a future, a future line—respect them, discover their message and ecology and reframe them.

1. Have the person make an image of something mundane that he/she knows he/she will be doing 5, 10, 20 years from now.

2. Place these images at comfortable increments of time (every 3-10 years) along an ecological trajectory in space.

3. Connect these "dots" so that you have the skeleton of a future Time Line.

4. Ask the person to identify several criteria (values) that he/she

knows will continue to be important 5, 10, 20, 30 years, etc. from now. Direct him/her to make an abstract image that symbolizes each of those values.

5. Have the person place these images at various places along the future Time Line. Put the image of each value in several places along the line. This begins the process of "fleshing" out the skeleton line—making it more "real"/"concrete." You can have the person put images of doing things he/she knows he'll be doing—going to the beach, fishing, reading, visiting friends, etc. Be careful not to make these images too specific. Not what specific beach, or which specific friends—after all, this is the future and we can't know exactly what will happen.

Note: Be sure to give these images specific submodalities that distinguish them from the past and that feel comfortable and motivating.

Time Lines can significantly affect how a person organizes him/ herself, plans and accomplishes goals. Time Lines affect motivation, self-esteem and emotions. If a person does not have a future Time Line, or it is blocked, or merges with the past line, he/she may be depressed, self-destructive, obsessive or lack motivation or be unable to plan the future, organize work and succeed.

APPENDIX 5

BOUNDARIES

Boundaries are those distinctions we make between our inside and outside world, between ourselves and others, and between different contexts or types of situations.

Boundaries make distinctions, maintain separateness and individuality, **and** are permeable. They allow the exchange of information and emotions; they enable connection without merging.

When self-other boundaries are too rigid, they become walls. There is little exchange, especially of emotions, because boundaries are no longer permeable. Another person's inner emotional state will have little effect on one's own self.

In contrast, when self-other boundaries are excessively diffuse, there is a loss of separateness—a loss of boundaries. Then merging can occur—overidentification with the loss of one's cognitive abilities and useful objective observations.

In order to have boundaries, one must have:

- An appreciation of and sensitivity to the to differences as well as sameness of people, memories, situations.
- An awareness and connection to one's physical body; some internally located value.
- An ability to identify with and participate in another's emotions while maintaining one's own sense of separateness.
- Development of an inner observer.
- An experience of the relationship of time and self as an evolving, everchanging process.
- An ability to maintain peripheral vision and hearing, to

see the larger picture and maintain awareness of the whole rather than be trapped in the perceptions of a part representing or becoming the whole.

In examining the **Enneagram**, we note a general tendency in terms of boundary distinctions (boundaries, no boundaries, walls) within each triad. The relationship of **Twos/Threes/Fours** to the safety/security issue is tied up with identity, which often results in these core personality types having no boundaries. The relationship of **Fives/Sixes/Sevens** to the safety/security issue is tied up with fear, which often results in these core personality types having walls. The relationship of **Eights/Nines/Ones** to the safety/security issue is tied up with anger, which results in these core personality types bouncing back and forth between having walls and having no boundaries.

Boundaries Model^{SM}
Based on the work of Anné Linden

Boundary Definition

Boundaries are those distinctions we make between our Inside and Outside world, between Ourselves and Others, and between different Contexts or types of situations.

Properties of Boundaries

Permeability (allows for **bi-lateral** exchange of information), flexibility, and maintenance of separation.

Boundary Distinctions

1. **Boundaries**: Boundaries allow for the exchange of information and emotions while maintaining separateness and individuality. They enable connection without merging—without loss of self.

2. **No Boundaries**: When boundaries are excessively diffuse, there

is loss of separation and distinction. This results in merging with the other, overidentification with another and the loss of self—one's sense of self as unique and separate and one's cognitive and perceptual objective observations. This can be desirable in certain situations but limiting in others.

3. **Walls**: When boundaries are too rigid they become walls. There is little exchange, especially of emotions because there is no longer permeability. This results in another's inner emotional state having little impact on one's own state. In general, walls make connections with others impossible and support rigid ideas and beliefs about self and the world; growth and evolvement become very difficult. Sometimes walls are helpful when outside events or emotions are overwhelming and they are the only way one has to maintain separation and protect oneself.

Note: What is most important about these distinctions is that one is aware of them and has choice about having boundaries, walls, or no boundaries.

Types of Boundaries

1. **Internal/External**: Distinctions between what is me and what is not me—What is part of my internal experience and what is outside me, the external world. Skin is a fundamental example of an Internal/External Boundary. Skin has the properties of Boundaries: permeability, flexibility and makes and keeps distinctions and separation.

2. **Self/Other**: Distinctions between self and significant others. The ability to have and maintain the difference between your emotions and someone else's, your thoughts and someone else's. Feeling for a friend's pain and knowing it is not yours is an example of self/other boundaries.

3. **Contextual Boundaries**: Distinctions made between different types of situations, with different rules for appropriate behavior and expectations.

a. **People**: Type or categories of people; authority figures, children, police, priests/rabbis, etc.
b. **Activities**: Different types of activities; parenting, working, playing, etc.
c. **Place**: Different types of places; office, bedroom, church, nightclub, etc.
d. **Gender**: Sexual distinctions; male, female.
e. **Time**: Distinctions dependent on time; Saturday night, holidays, middleage, etc.

Cognitive And Perceptual Developmental Abilities Necessary For Developing And Maintaining Boundaries

1. **Ego Strength**: Sense of self as a separate entity with own values—located inside rather than outside self.

2. **Self as a Process**: A dynamic relationship with Time allows one to experience self as a dynamic ever-changing process rather than a static object. Time allows one to go back and do something again.

3. **Notice difference**: Ability to notice differences—how things, people, information are different as well as the same.

4. **Observer Self**: Ability to be aware of self—to step outside and be an objective observer of self—self awareness as a separate being.

5. **Identify With Others**: Ability to shift point of view to that of the other person. Literally to step inside another's shoes.

The Boundaries Process^{SM}
Based on the work of Anné Linden

The "How To's" of Boundaries

1. **Simultaneous Thinking**: Noticing and appreciating sameness and difference. Paying attention to how someone or something is the same as you, as well as different from you: similar and different emotions, ideas, opinions, behaviors, etc. Attending to how a situation is the same as a past situation or the same as your expectations, as well as different.

2. **Strong Connection To Your Body**: Maintaining a physical sense and awareness of your body—connecting to the ground (chair) underneath you, to your breathing, your center of gravity. Physically connecting to your body as separate and distinct from anything else around.

3. **Peripheral Vision and/or Hearing**: Literally, maintaining your peripheral seeing and hearing. It is usually enough to maintain either peripheral seeing or peripheral hearing. This means that while you are looking or listening to someone or something, you can also—without moving your eyes or head—see or hear whatever else is around you **and** the object of your immediate attention, at the same time.

Submodality Distinctions

Boundaries	Walls	No Boundaries
• Panoramic (Peripheral) Visual • Panoramic (Peripheral) Auditory	• Small, framed Images	• Tunnel Vision • Tunnel Hearing
• Life-like color	• Dissociated • Black & White	• Associated • Distortion of foreground
• 3 Dimensional • Normal	• 2 Dimensional • Distance:	to background: foreground

(proportional) relationship of foreground to background in Visual & Auditory Systems	Images & External (environ- mental) sounds far away	emphasized in Visual and/or Auditory Systems
•Movement between Dissociated and Associated	•Internal Auditory (meta chatter) distorted— faster tempo & louder than normal	•Figure in figure/ground relationship is often brighter, louder, clearer, larger •Distance: fore- ground images & sounds closer than normal

Peripheral Process I

1. **Look at something directly** in front of you. Put your hands about two feet in front of you and about two and a half feet apart, on the same level with your eyes, so that they frame whatever you are looking at.

2. **Without changing your focus,** begin to slowly move your hands further out and toward a position opposite your shoulders.

3. **Stop as soon as you can no longer** see your hands. Go back to where you can see them and try to "stretch" your peripheral vision. You can "wiggle" your fingers to stretch your peripheral vision.

4. **To do this with hearing** you listen to someone talking. First, concentrate just on his/her words and tonality, then add awareness of the sounds in the room, other people's voices, etc.— so that your hearing includes peripheral. (**Note:** This is an ability everyone has. In order to strengthen it, just practice the above exercise.)

Peripheral Process II

1. **Think of a situation** with another person that happens with some frequency and is damaging to your self-esteem.

2. **Connect to your body**—maintain a physical sense of self.

3. **Watch movie**: See self in the movie. Make it a series of small, framed stills, 2-D, black and white.

4. **Watch movie again**: See self and do peripheral vision. (If necessary, put up hands to frame your image and move them out to periphery in order to guide your vision. Do not look directly at the periphery.)

5. **Watch movie again**—as though you are there inside experience (not seeing self) *and* maintain peripheral vision, connection to body, and notice sameness and differences. Ask self, "Whose values am I using?" "What can I learn?" If the values you are using are your own, ask self, "How can I be different in the future?"

Note: For some people peripheral vision is easier to strengthen than peripheral hearing. You can also work on both peripheral hearing and vision.

The result of this process is often that people experience the "Big Picture"; they can literally begin to see the relationship of the main object of their attention with other information; the situation doesn't "loom" over them while they still remain connected. There is more balance between various elements in the experience. It brings everything into perspective; there is no longer a distortion between foreground and background—things are in proportion. This is because of the presence of boundaries which maintain separateness with permeability, allowing the awareness and exchange of other information and emotions. This produces simultaneous thinking: separation and connectedness, sameness and difference.

APPENDIX 6

RECOMMENDED BOOKS

THE ENNEAGRAM

The Enneagram (Helen Palmer; Harper & Row)
Ennea-Type Structures: Self Analysis For The Seeker
(Claudio Naranjo, M.D.; Gateways/DHHB, Inc.)
The Gurdjieff Work (Kathleen Riordan-Speeth; Simon & Schuster)
Personality Types: Using The Enneagram For Self-Discovery
(Don Richard Riso; Houghton Mifflin)
*Understanding The Enneagram: The Practical Guide To
Personality Types* (Don Richard Riso; Houghton Mifflin)

NEUROLINGUISTIC PROGRAMMING

Beliefs: Pathways To Health & Well-Being (Robert Dilts,
Tim Hallbom & Suzie Smith; Metamorphous Press)
Influencing With Integrity (Genie Z. Laborde; Syntony
Publishing)
*Introducing Neurolinguistic Programming: The New
Psychology of Personal Excellence* (Joseph O'Connor
& John Seymour; The Aquarian Press)
Magic of NLP Demystified (Byron Lewis & Frank Pucelik;
Metamorphous Press)
Practical Magic (Steven Lankton, A.C.S.W.; Grinder, DeLozier
& Associates)
Reframing (Richard Bandler & John Grinder; Real People Press)
The Structure of Magic, Vol. I & II (Richard Bandler & John
Grinder; Science & Behavior Books)
Using Your Brain For A Change (Richard Bandler; Real
People Press)

About The Authors

ANNÉ LINDEN completed undergraduate work at Columbia University and received her graduate degree in psychology from Goddard College. She was trained in Gestalt, Transactional Analysis, and Psychodrama, and studied and worked personally with Laura Perls, Dr. Milton Erickson, and the originators of Neurolinguistic Programming. A psychotherapist since 1977, she has maintained an active practice in addition to training and supervising therapists. Anné is the founder and director of the NLP Center for Psychotherapy and the New York Training Institute for NLP. She has personally designed and taught over 100 certification programs during the last fifteen years. Anné has lectured, trained, and consulted throughout the United States, Europe and Israel to a wide variety of professionals and organizations. She has three children and has homes in Cape Cod, Massachusetts and New York City.

MURRAY SPALDING was raised in Kentucky and earned a B.A. and an M.A. in Dance at Sarah Lawrence College. She combined her interests in philosophy with studies in psychology and metaphysics. With this background, her choreographic works began to evolve into esoteric, serious modern dances, intended not to entertain but to enlighten. Paralleling directing and touring for twenty years with her own dance company—Murray Spalding Dance Theatre—she became a therapist for artists, counseling them in both their careers and psychological issues. Through combining hypnotherapy, Neurolinguistic Programming, Past Life therapy, and the Enneagram, Murray has integrated these methodologies into tremendously successful changework. She lives in the Soho neighborhood of New York City with her husband and has four step-children and two Asian Leopardette cats.

Anné Linden   Murray Spalding

Metamorphous Press

Metamorphous Press is a publisher of books and other media providing resources for personal growth and positive change. MP publishes leading-edge ideas that help people strengthen their unique talents and discover that we are responsible for our own realities.

Many of our titles center around Neurolinguistic Programming (NLP) and the Enneagram. These are exciting, practical, and powerful models that connect you to observable patterns of behavior and communication and the processes that underlie them.

Metamorphous Press provides selections in many useful subject areas such as communication, health and fitness, education, business and sales, therapy, selections for young persons, and other subjects of general and specific interest. Our products are available in fine bookstores around the world.

Our distributors for North America are:

Bookpeople	Moving Books	the distributors
Ingram	New Leaf	Sage Book Distributors
M.A.P.S.	Pacific Pipeline	

For those of you overseas, we are distributed by:

Airlift (UK, Western Europe)
Specialist Publications (Australia)

New selections are added regularly and availability and prices change, so call for a current catalog or to be put on our mailing list. If you have difficulty finding our products in your favorite bookstore, or if you prefer to order by mail, we will be happy to make our books and other products available to you directly. Please call or write us at:

Metamorphous Press

P.O. Box 10616   Portland, OR 97296-0616
TEL (503) 228-4972
FAX (503) 223-9117

TOLL FREE ORDERING
1-800-937-7771

Metamorphous Advanced Product Services

Metamorphous Advanced Product Services (M.A.P.S.) is the master distributor for Metamorphous Press and other fine publishers.

M.A.P.S. offers books, cassettes, videos, software, and miscellaneous products in the following subjects: Business & Sales, Children, Education, Enneagram, Health (including Alexander Technique and Rolfing), Hypnosis, Personal Development, Psychology (including Neurolinguistic Programming), and Relationships/Sexuality.

If you cannot find our books at your favorite bookstore, you can order directly from M.A.P.S.

TO ORDER OR REQUEST A FREE CATALOG:

MAIL   M.A.P.S.
P.O. Box 10616
Portland, OR 97296-0616

FAX   (503) 223-9117

CALL   Toll free 1-800-937-7771

ALL OTHER BUSINESS:

CALL   (503) 228-4972